D1124493

DATE DUE

May 11			
GAYLORD			PRINTED IN U.S.A.

Sweet Bamboo

The Tom Leung family in 1909. The children are Taft (baby), Lillie, and Louise (the author).

A Memoir

of a

Chinese

American

Family

Sweet Bamboo

Louise Leung Larson

With a Foreword by Shirley Hune
and a Postscript by Jane Leung Larson

UNIVERSITY OF CALIFORNIA PRESS
Berkeley   Los Angeles   London

University of California Press
Berkeley and Los Angeles, California

University of California Press, Ltd.
London, England

© 1989 by Louise Leung Larson
First California Paperback, 2001

Library of Congress Cataloging-in-Publication Data

Larson, Louise Leung.
    Sweet bamboo : a memoir of a Chinese American
family / Louise Leung Larson ; with a foreword
by Shirley Hune and a postscript by Jane Leung
Larson.
        p.   cm.
    Originally published: Los Angeles, Calif. :
Chinese Historical Society of Southern
California, 1990.
    ISBN 0-520-23078-7 (pbk. : alk. paper)
    1. Chinese Americans — California — Los Angeles.
2. Liang family. I. Title: Memoir of a Chinese American family. II. Title.

    F869.L89 C53 2001
    979.4'94004951—dc21   2001027343

Printed in the United States of America

08   07   06   05   04   03   02   01
10   9   8   7   6   5   4   3   2   1

Contents

Foreword

Situating *Sweet Bamboo* in Chinese American History

SHIRLEY HUNE

Louise Leung Larson's "story of Papa and Mama (accent on the second syllable, Chinese style) and their nine children" is a narrative full of richly textured vignettes about the everyday life of a large, upper-middle-class, multigenerational Chinese American family in Los Angeles from the 1900s to the 1950s. Its presentation is enhanced with family photos and flavored by Cantonese phrases — such as "fo yer" (salted bean curd), "Bok Foo" (paternal uncle), "fung sup" (rheumatism), and being "mung jung" (cross or irritable). Most appropriately, this work, first published in 1989, is being reprinted around the centenary of the parents' departure from the village of Gum Jook (Sweet Bamboo) and their settlement in the Gold Mountain (United States). From it, as from many American immigrant sagas, we learn about dreams and disappointments, of growing up straddling different cultural worlds, of food habits, holiday celebrations, and the personalities of relatives. Yet this story is also different.

Sweet Bamboo is distinct in its disclosure of the privileged lifestyle of the Tom Leung family — with its eight American-born children (the ninth and eldest had died in China), large home in a predominantly white neighborhood, servants, and material goods — in a period of legal racial discrimination against the Chinese. The book provides intimate portraits of family relations and of social interactions with the larger society, as employers — of whites, blacks, and Chinese in both the family herbalist business and the household — and as members of a leisure class. Such a lifestyle was vastly different from that of other Chinese Americans in this period, most of whom were unskilled workers living in Chinatowns. Even where laws permitted otherwise or could be circumvented, many Chinese immigrants maintained "split households," transnational families comprised of married "bachelors" locked into low-paying menial jobs in the United States and wives and children who remained in China as an economic strategy for their joint survival.[1]

The family memoir begins in China's Kwangtung Province, Sun Duck County, Gum Jook Herng, about thirty-one miles south of Canton. Here both Mama (Wong Bing Woo) and Papa (Tom Cherng How) were born in 1875 and raised in relatively comfortable households in villages across the river from one another. After an arranged marriage in 1898, Papa, joined later by Mama, settled in Los Angeles, where three daughters and five sons (the latter Papa named after American presidents) were born between 1902 and 1917. The author of this family saga is the second daughter, "Mamie" Louise Leung Larson, a woman of independent spirit who shocked her family by marrying outside the Chinese community. In 1926, at age 21, she became the first Asian American reporter for a major American newspaper, the *Los Angeles Record;* later, as a noted journalist, she covered national events and was a recognized pioneer among Chinese American women.

Larson describes how Tom Cherng How developed a successful herbalist business with a broad-based Chinese and non-Chinese clientele, using Tom Leung as a business name. In time, to reduce confusion over their surname, the children adopted Leung as the family name in place of Tom — their proper surname by the Chinese order of names. Papa immersed himself in American life while retaining his interest in Chinese politics. For example, he hired the son of a white business owner from across the street to teach him English, which he never fully mastered, while continuing his longtime devotion to Kang You-wei's efforts to politically reform China. Papa took great care that Mama, who unbound her feet after the birth of her first American-born child, had fashionable American clothes and someone to advise her on how to wear them. To fulfill his dream of a big modern house, he purchased a lot in a non-Chinese residential area under eldest daughter Lillie's name — as a non-citizen and Chinese, Papa could not own property. There, at 1619 West Pico, with space for the herbalist business on the first floor, Papa had a fifteen-room home built and carefully chose all its furnishings.

Over the years, Mama had Chinese and black cooks to prepare family meals, especially rich banquet-like dinners — Papa's preference. White nannies assisted with childcare and "colored" women washed the clothes. Mama enjoyed smoking a water pipe and joined Papa after dinner in their leather chairs in the second-floor parlor to read books and Chinese newspapers and discuss things together. Mama was the heart of the household and served as the "middle-man" relaying the children's wishes and school progress to Papa, who was indulgent and respected, but distant. She had her own interest in the modernization movement in China, and with Papa frequently hosted events in their home and at lavish public banquets to aid Kang You-wei's political movement.

The eight American-born children had a relatively carefree and racially unsegregated life through childhood and adolescence, with household staff to take care of their daily needs. They celebrated both American and Chinese holidays with elaborate meals and gifts, but oftentimes resented being different from their schoolmates, for example by having to eat Chinese meals three times a day instead of simpler American food. Papa provided a series of tutors to teach the children Chinese, but their efforts were largely unsuccessful. While many Chinese customs were followed, such as having a clean house and not cutting one's hair on Chinese New Year, the children also took music lessons and played tennis. The family had a "talking machine" with a horn for the jazz and dance records enjoyed by the second generation; Papa listened to classical music and Mama loved Chinese opera. In addition, the household engaged in many leisure activities, like weekends at beach resorts and Sunday picnics. As the older children started college, their large home — "1619" —

was a site for American-born youth activities, including meetings of the Chinese Students Club of the University of Southern California and parties with dancing and live bands.

The family's class advantage did not entirely protect them from racism in the larger society, however. For example, the success of Chinese herbalists in Los Angeles drew the attention of the American Medical Association and the Board of Medical Examiners. Accused of practicing medicine without a license, Papa and other herbalists were frequently arrested by the police and required to pay fines before resuming their valued trade. Daughter 'Mamie" (Louise), the author, also recalled rebuffs while growing up, including the humiliation of being turned away with her friends from a dance hall and of being treated with suspicion and mistaken for Japanese during World War II. And Taft, the eldest American-born son, had his dream of becoming a professional musician ended after being denied union membership — a necessity for employment — because of his race.

Mostly, however, *Sweet Bamboo* describes a life of relative abundance with a mixture of Chinese and American lifestyles — until the family was abruptly "catapulted from prosperity into poverty" by Papa's sudden death in 1931 at age fifty-six and the subsequent decline of the herbalist business and impact of the depression. It was the end of their carefree days. During the 1930s and World War II, with four sons and a grandson in uniform, Mama emerged as the matriarch who kept the family together through hardships. Her house was the center, with the eight children, now adults, making sacrifices for the family's survival, including dropping out of college and taking jobs at great distances to send money home. By the 1950s the children and grandchildren visited Mama regularly, sometimes daily. A few lived with her or moved close by long after establishing their own households. Mama died in 1957 having never learned English, and her death marked the end of this memoir and the end of an era for the Tom Leung family.

The author informs us in a brief epilogue that the extended family was in its fifth generation when the book was first published in 1989. With much intermarriage during the third and fourth generations, the family's sense of being Chinese had diminished. More than a decade later, the author's daughter, Jane Leung Larson, provides an update of the family in a postscript to this second edition. Presently, descendants of the Tom Leung family are of mixed European and Japanese ethnicity as well as Chinese, and are solidly middle class rather than upper-middle class. And while a few family members have retained an interest in things Chinese or Chinese American, others have not. Larson also shares with us her two visits to China in the 1990s, including her return to the village of Sweet Bamboo where the family memoir begins, and recounts the impact of the Communist revolution on the lives of Mama's and Papa's relatives there. Most importantly, she informs us of the discovery of her grandfather's classical Chinese library and papers documenting overseas Chinese efforts to politically reform China, materials now available to scholars at UCLA's East Asian Library. The family still has multigenerational gatherings, now held at the home of Holly, the youngest daughter of Tom Cherng How and Wong Bing Woo.

"Mamie" Louise Leung Larson saw this book as "a collection of memories of a family brought up amidst conflicting Chinese and American cultures." The family saga was her effort to instill interest among the fourth and fifth generations about their roots in China. I view it as more than a memoir. It is also a historical document about a particular time and place in Chinese American and U.S. history.

This highly readable volume sheds new light on the diversity of early Chinese America and its family life, thus challenging many stereotypical conceptions about the community in the first half of the twentieth century. As one of the few studies of privileged Chinese households in the United States in the early 1900s, it illuminates a little-known way of being immigrant and second-generation Chinese Americans.[2] While much attention has deservedly been given in the historical literature to the "bachelor society" and the struggles of working-class Chinese immigrants, this book reveals that a middle-class lifestyle — and some might view the Leung household as having an upper-class lifestyle (and the arrogance that went with it) — existed for some Chinese Americans in the early decades of the twentieth century. Greater attention to different groups of Chinese immigrants and the experiences of middle-class and upper-middle-class life before World War II enhances our understanding of the range of Chinese American lives and uncovers long-standing class differences within the community.

Sweet Bamboo also contributes to economic and racial history in its details of Chinese herbalist practices and its attention to Chinese professionals before the 1930s, a neglected topic. The window it offers onto that world discloses the racialized complexities of building an herbalist business: for example, the need to wear Chinese apparel to connote expertise but also to hire white receptionists to assist with non-Chinese clientele. A recent study argues that Chinese herbalists utilized skills and knowledge derived from their ethnic culture to create a profession in the United States that served different racial and ethnic groups. In resisting the racially defined occupational positions of the day, they made a significant contribution to the health care of the region, a fact that transforms our understanding of the role of the Chinese in the American West.[3]

The memoir also reveals the efforts and ambiguities of one family's transnational relations with its homeland. To what extent did the Tom Leung family maintain close and regular contacts with China? How frequently did family members move between two or more locations?[4] Papa's 1921 trip to China to investigate educational opportunities for his sons there suggested a strong desire to maintain their Chinese heritage. However, he found the schools unsatisfactory, and this goal went unfulfilled. Mama rejected pressures from Papa's relatives for the household to return to China after his death, concluding that she valued her independence from the extended family and that she and her children belonged in the United States. And what hold did China have on its emigrants in this period? The participation of Chinese immigrants in homeland affairs at the turn of the twentieth century has yet to be adequately documented by scholars. Larson provides some observations of the efforts of Papa, Mama, and other Chinese immigrants to support political change in China.[5]

The author also informs us of how her family dealt with race, class, gender, and cultural differences in this period. The notion that Chinese American lives were wholly racially segregated or self-contained with other co-ethnics in the early part of the twentieth century is dispelled here. For example, the descriptions of employer-employee race relations and other racial dynamics among whites, blacks, and other Asians initiated and experienced by the Tom Leung household extend our understanding of racial mixing in the

American West during these years. Larson's emphasis on Mama's life in China and the United States and on the activities of the daughters also fills a gap and helps to balance a Chinese American history that is biased toward a male experience. Hence the family memoir contributes to a multicultural history of the United States, showing how interracial, intergenerational, gendered, cultural, and class dynamics were lived every day.

Sweet Bamboo is most revealing about gender and family roles. For example, Papa sought to be very American in his dress and activities and was in many ways a modern man for the time, yet reverted to tradition in securing a concubine ("gip see") during his 1921 China trip. And Mama was not simply a "good Chinese wife." She gave Papa an ultimatum — stay in China with the concubine and send money to support the family, or come home without her. Her many actions before and (especially) after his death to ensure the family's survival underscored her influence on the household. On children's roles, for example, Lillie, as the eldest American-born child, typically at a very early age served as the English translator for Papa on many business matters, and later could be depended upon to drive everyone around in the family car. Lillie bore enormous responsibilities on behalf of the household and continued to do so long after she had established her own family and was holding down an important job in the Chinese consulate as well. Gender and family roles here were not fixed or linear, that is, moving from traditional to modern, but complex and fluid. Mama and Papa were flexible in their roles and activities, sometimes traditionally Chinese, sometimes more American, and oftentimes at once Chinese and American and in between.

The author also provides keen observations of the second generation's adaptation to two cultures and of the formation of a Chinese American sensibility, albeit from an economically advantaged position. Larson acknowledges that at that time the family was *class* conscious (an attitude learned in part from Papa and one that distanced them from other Americans, including the Chinatown Chinese) but not particularly *race* conscious, as was shown in their empathy for — but not outrage about — interned Japanese Americans. Those who study second-generation Chinese Americans of the post–World War II era or of the post-1965 immigration period will find both continuities and differences in home life and interactions with the world outside the family. The details of daily life, such as meal times, fun times, and times with Mama and Papa, and the discussions of larger social practices, such as making friends and getting jobs, are engaging and reveal both the possibilities and limitations of the period and the family's status. For the most part, the American-born children sought to be American, accommodated being Chinese, and in some ways offered little resistance to their situations. And, in spite of their Americanization, family members even as adults inhabited a multigenerational compound together at "1619" (West Pico) from the 1930s to the 1950s, a practice the author observed as being so like "the Chinese way" and so unlike "the American way."

A memoir presents its participants as subjects of history and agents of cultural change. Here two generations of the Tom Leung family actively interject themselves into American life. They are seen making decisions as to the way they seek to live, whether it be emigrating to the United States, maintaining Chinese food habits, promoting the herbal business through newspaper ads and cards to patients, visiting the 1915 World's Fair in San Francisco, holding dance parties in their home, pooling meager resources to survive and pay off debts after Papa's death, or seeking job opportunities in the arts field.

A memoir also has its weaknesses. This family narrative has many of those moments in which one wants to know more — gaps identified by the author as well. As Larson notes, if only the family had thought to ask Papa or Mama about that, or if only those letters had been saved . . . These empty spaces should encourage more of us to conduct oral histories with our own families and with others — "talk story" — and to gather up those letters, photos, and other mementos and view them as historical documents and material culture. Collections of observations and reminiscences grow more powerful when situated in a historical context and analyzed for their meaning within a larger whole. Each family story is part of a larger history. Historians, social scientists, and others can help draw the connections and place individual and group lives within a larger collective history.

Louise Leung Larson's *Sweet Bamboo* is a family memoir to be enjoyed for its personalities, observations, and vignettes. It is more than a work for the general public. It makes a contribution to the history of the Chinese in the United States and resonates with themes of interest to contemporary scholars, such as transnational linkages, racial intersections, ethnic entrepreneurship, class, gender, and generational dynamics, ethnic identity, cultural adaptation, accommodation and resistance, and tradition and change. It also has a place in local history, providing details of being Chinese American in Los Angeles. Mostly, it is a story about the everyday lives of people who care for one another through abundance and hardships: a lot like other families, and yet different — for they were privileged at a time when most other Chinese Americans were not.

NOTES

1. Evelyn Nakano Glenn, "Split Household, Small Producer and Dual Wage Earner: An Analysis of Chinese-American Family Strategies," *Journal of Marriage and the Family* 45:1 (February 1983): 35–46.

2. For a detailed study of another Chinese American family in Los Angeles of this period, but one that began less well-to-do and was based on an interracial household with the marriage of Fong See, the patriarch, and Letticie Pruett in 1897, see Lisa See, *On Gold Mountain: The One-Hundred-Year Odyssey of a Chinese-American Family* (New York: St. Martin's Press, 1995). Some aspects of the lives of middle-class Chinese American women in San Francisco during the first half of the twentieth century are discussed in Judy Yung, *Unbound Feet: A Social History of Chinese Women in San Francisco* (Berkeley and Los Angeles: University of California Press, 1995).

3. Haiming Liu, "The Resilience of Ethnic Culture: Chinese Herbalists in the American Medical Profession," *Journal of Asian American Studies* 1:2 (June 1998): 173–191.

4. The opportunities for Chinese Americans to be transnational subjects and maintain transnational households are vastly different in the twenty-first century with the development of Asian capitalism and the contemporary global economy as compared to the colonial era at the turn of the twentieth century. On Chinese transnationalism between Taishan County, South China and the United States, 1882–1943, see Madeline Y. Hsu, *Dreaming of Gold, Dreaming of Home* (Stanford: Stanford University Press, 2000). For a discussion of contemporary privileged transnational Chinese,

see Aihwa Ong, "On the Edge of Empires: Flexible Citizenship among Chinese in Diaspora," *Positions* 1:3 (Winter 1993): 745–778.

5. More details of the activities of overseas Chinese in the Chinese Empire Reform Association can be found in the Tom Leung papers and documents located by the family after the publication of *Sweet Bamboo*. For information on the Tom Leung papers as primary source materials for Kang Youwei and the Chinese Empire Reform Association, see the following works of Jane Leung Larson: "New Source Materials on Kang Youwei and the Baohuanghui: The Tan Zhangxiao (Tom Leung) Collection of Letters and Documents at UCLA's East Asian Library," in *Chinese America: History and Perspectives, 1993* (San Francisco, CA: Chinese Historical Society, 1993), 151–198; and "The Tom Leung Papers: New Source Materials on the Chinese Empire Reform Association," in *Origins and Destinations: 41 Essays on Chinese America* (Los Angeles, CA: Chinese Historical Society of Southern California and UCLA Asian American Studies Center, 1994), 243–256.

Foreword to the First Edition

This is the story of Papa and Mama (accent on the second syllable, Chinese style) and their nine children, eight of whom were born and raised in Los Angeles. It depicts what life was like for one Chinese-American family, the Tom Leungs, from the turn of the century to the present.

Mama provided all the material on her and Papa's lives in China and their early years in this country. The language barrier made complete, in-depth communication impossible, but she spent hours with me and my former husband, the late Arnold B. Larson, who had an abiding interest in the family history.

In 1940, Arnold goaded all the Leungs to write down their memories of family life at 903 S. Olive and 1619 W. Pico, the family homesteads. None of us considered this of any importance. Who would care, we thought. The best response came from my brother Monroe, who at 24, produced a lively, humorous, and sometimes moving document. Many passages are quoted in these pages. Diaries written by my brother William provided more material. Arnold interviewed many family friends and associates and took notes on family happenings.

My daughter, Jane Leung Larson, wrote a thesis at Reed College in Portland, Oregon, in 1967, entitled "The Social Environment of a Chinese-American Family as Explored Through Personal Documents." It was based on the Leung family and was the result of much painstaking, scholarly research. It provided valuable source material. (Of the entire extended family, Jane is the only one who voluntarily studied Chinese and continues to do so, and speaks fairly good Mandarin. She is now executive director of the Northwest China Council in Portland. Working with her teacher, Charles Liu of Portland State University, Jane has overseen the translation of scores of letters written by relatives in China to Papa and Mama.)

For years, the notes and data were filed away and forgotten. But after several trips to China, I felt that the story of Papa and Mama, two extraordinary people, and the family they raised in Gold Mountain, deserved to be told. There are probably omissions and inaccuracies, but this work is not a scholarly, researched dissertation. It is a collection of memories of a family brought up amidst conflicting Chinese and American cultures.

It is a great honor and distinction that the Chinese Historical Society of Southern California has chosen to publish the Tom Leung family history. I owe special thanks to Angi Ma Wong, president of the Society, Suellen Cheng, Munson Kwok, Kipham Kan, Don Loo, Barbara Larson, Diana Wong and Chung Wong for the many long hours spent on this project. And I am profoundly grateful to my sister, Holly Lee, who supported the publication of this story by reallocating a portion of the memorial funds donated to the Society for her husband, Dr. Edward Lee.

Louise Leung Larson

CHINA BEGINNINGS

CHAPTER I

Mama's Childhood

Papa and Mama were born in 1875, in the first year of the reign of the Manchu Emperor Kuang-hsu. The pewter incense burner on my desk contains some dirt I brought home from the area of their birth in Kwangtung Province, Sun Duck County, Gum Jook Herng (I am using Cantonese, not Mandarin, phonetic spelling). It is located 50 kilometers (about 31 miles) south of Canton.

My daughter Jane and I made a trip there in 1977. The Gum Jook (Sweet Bamboo) Hydraulic Power Plant was then the showplace of Sun Duck County, and it was because of the plant that our guide-interpreter, a young girl named Lu, was able to locate our ancestral birthplace. The area is very rural, with terraced hillsides and low mountains in the background. The rich soil produces wonderful crops of rice and mulberry bushes. The people who live there are members of the Dragon River People's Commune. One production brigade (village) is named Jo Tan (left bank) where Papa was born, and the other is called Yo Tan (right bank) where Mama lived.

The plant is built on the left bank. We stood there, looking across the river and wondered where Mama's house had been. I could well

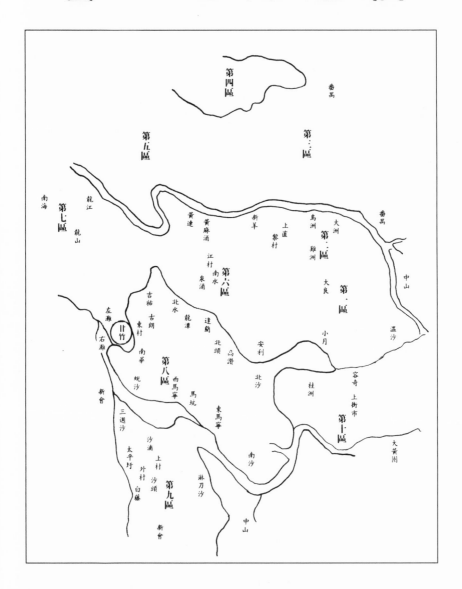

Map of Sun Duck County, Canton, China.
The village of Sweet Bamboo is enclosed by the circle.

understand why she always spoke so longingly of her girlhood home; it was still so beautiful and tranquil. Of course, she lived in another world from the one we were seeing. There is a vast chasm between life under the Manchus and life under communism. Not only was the whole fabric of society transformed, but even the rivers, we were told, had been "tamed" and channeled. There probably are descendants of our parents still living in our native village, according to our host at the plant — the Toms at Jo Tan, and the Wongs at Yo Tan. Perhaps one day we will find them.

Mama was the youngest of four children. She had two sisters and one brother. Her father, Wong Mei Pun, was a wealthy exporter of sharks' fins. His firm, named "Kwong Fung Wah," was based in Hong Kong and had 20 employees. He came home, a day's boat ride away, only a few times a year, on such occasions as New Year's, the Moon and Dragon Boat festivals, family weddings and funerals. Mama's mother was his second wife who died when Mama was only three (four in Chinese counting). Mama remembered nothing of her mother and didn't even have a picture of her, or of any member of her family. She had one vivid memory of her mother's death. Her Aunt Beautiful Pearl slapped her because she had not cried and had not been at her mother's deathbed. The slap was not a punishment, but a custom. It was meted out to all family members who were not at the deathbed.

After her mother's death, Mama and her sisters and brother went to live in her father's ancestral home in the nearby village of Sweet Bamboo (Gum Jook), a half day's boat journey from Canton. The immediate household consisted of the grandmother, two uncles and their wives, four cousins and their spouses, and numerous children. The grandfather had died by the time Mama became a member of the household. He had been a tea exporter in Shanghai who lived with concubines. He rarely came home. The grandmother told Mama his business had gone bankrupt. With money loaned him by a relative, he had opened exchange houses in Peking, Shanghai, and Hong Kong. The chain of banks, called Sun Wo Tai, was still in existence in the early 1920's, according to Mama.

The household grew and Mama said there were eventually 25 persons, including 12 children. The family compound consisted of 10 grey brick buildings with curving Chinese roofs, with a family unit occupying each house. There were guest houses for visitors, separate ones for men and women. An eight-foot-high wall of grey brick surrounded the compound. A barred gate, attended by servants, opened into a courtyard. This elaborate layout was called "Gim Sing Tong," meaning "Built With Money Earned by Industry," and covered ground equal to an average American city block.

Parklike gardens graced the estate. There were trees of all kinds: kumquat, apricot, lemon, lichee nut, loquat, and tangerine. Flowers grew profusely. One, an orange flower called *dan gway*, was as tall as the buildings and bloomed in September. Its fragrance permeated the area even beyond the compound gate.

Each family member had a servant whose sole duty was to attend to his or her needs. Mama had a nurse *(goo mah)* and later on a maid *(mui jay)*. For each family unit, there were cooks, washwomen, boys to fetch wood and water, and gardeners. Grandmother was the matriarch of this large household and supervised Mama's upbringing. Mama led a life of ease, as she often told us. She remembered those days with a roseate view, despite the lack of running water, indoor plumbing, a heating system, or electricity. Apparently, the lack of amenities was no hardship. There were servants galore to perform all the menial tasks.

Mama's leisurely day began at ten, when she rose and breakfasted on *jook* (rice gruel); she played until lunch, and played again until dinner. Bedtime for children was 9 or 10 p.m. The little girls played house with toy dishes and cooking utensils, but they had no dolls. There were games like blind man's bluff, hide and seek, and improvised shows where the children would dress up in their parents' clothes. Adults told them stories, mostly tales that dealt with ethical conduct and the necessity of filial devotion to parents. They were taught songs also. Mama recalled one about a boy who stole some water lilies. He rowed his boat into a pond thick with lilies, leaving behind him a cleft among the blossoms that exposed his theft.

Between the ages of 8 and 10, Mama learned to sew and embroider. Children did not go to school but were taught at home by tutors. In those days, it was thought education for girls was unnecessary, but Mama's father was progressive. He wanted his daughters to learn; so Mama was taught to read by a tutor at the age of eight, and to hold her brush and write characters. Later, she learned a little history and geography as well as some arithmetic, including use of the abacus. However, at age 12 her tutoring was stopped because her tutor was a man. Even with this limited education, Mama became an avid reader of novels and newspapers, and her calligraphy was unusually fine. Domestic chores such as cooking and house cleaning were outside the realm of the daughters in the Wong household. It was unthinkable that they would ever have to perform such menial tasks. Mama, many years later, as she cooked in our kitchen at 1619 W. Pico Street, would recall those halcyon days. *"Ho tahn"* (very luxurious), she would say nostalgically.

Ancestor worship was a family ritual at Gim Sing Tong. Polished wooden tablets inscribed with the names of the dead hung over a special table. A statue of Kwan Yin, goddess of mercy, had an honored place in the compound. Kwan Yin was one of Mama's favorite feminine characters. Another was Mook Lan, the famous Chinese heroine who went to war as a substitute for her aging father. Years later, Mama gave her first daughter, Lillie, the Chinese name Mook Lan.

The Wong girls were taught early how to beautify themselves. Mama was only five when her ears were pierced for earrings. On special holidays, she was allowed to use powder, rouge, and to color her lips with red-coated paper creased in accordion folds. Even now, in Communist China, nursery school children have their faces liberally made up when they appear in performances.

Probably the most traumatic event of Mama's childhood was the binding of her feet at age six. It would have been done earlier, but her mother's death required that three years pass before the binding. Aunt Beautiful Pearl bound the feet with cotton cloths. It was a tortuous process, and Mama cried with pain for months. Her feet were not unbound until after Lillie's birth. Mama was extremely sensitive on the subject of her bound feet. She was ashamed of them and didn't want to talk about the Chinese custom of lily feet. None of us ever saw her bare feet; she always wore white sox over them. Her bound feet were a lifelong burden, restricting her activities in every way.

When Mama was seven, her father married his third wife, a girl about 18 or 19. She came to live in the family compound. Mama called her *Ah Jieh* (sister). She eventually gave birth to three girls and a boy. Although *Ah Jieh* was Mama's stepmother, the grandmother continued to have supervision over Mama.

It was about this time that Mama first heard about America, or the Gold Mountain, as it was called by miners returning from California's great gold rush. On rare occasions, she saw European and American missionaries walking in the village. Their pale faces, yellow hair, narrow-creased pants and stiff collars seemed grotesque to the village children, who shouted *bok gway* (white ghosts) or *gway lo* (old ghosts) at them. Mama joined in the chorus of ridicule.

Mama recalled one event of her childhood about an uncle who died at the age of 14. The girl who had been chosen to marry him came to live at the grandmother's house. There was an elaborate ceremony in which the girl, just a child of 13, married the *gway* (ghost) of the dead boy. She even had to escort the body to the grave.

CHAPTER 2

Mama's Girlhood

Mama's "baby" name was Wong Way Yook, meaning "Cool Jade." This name was used only by family during her early years. There is a Chinese story that says Yang Kwei Fei, the famous concubine of 1200 years ago, used a piece of cool jade to dispel the heat from her body during the torrid summers. Mama got her name from this legend. Later, during her school years, her "baby" name was replaced with her permanent one, Bing Woo, meaning something like "Frosted Porcelain." This also had the connotation of tinkling ice, so welcome in the intense heat of South China.

At 15, Mama was deemed to be an adult. Until then, she had been on a "clear" diet of lean meat and vegetables. Now she was allowed to eat chicken, which had been prohibited because it was believed to "heat the blood." Mama continued all her life to have theories about chicken. We children were never allowed to eat it when we had a cold. She thought it would worsen the illness, unlike Jewish mothers who consider chicken soup the cure-all. At 15, Mama was also allowed to smoke a water pipe. She had been drinking tea since early childhood. She could now join the adults on their trips to the theatre two or three times a year to the nearby village. The ride was made in rickshas, and a midnight lunch was carried because the plays lasted all night. This was the beginning of her lifelong devotion to Chinese opera. As a grown-up young lady, Mama followed the routine of the women of Gim Sing Tong. She rose at noon, had her face washed with hot towels by her servant, and breakfasted on hot rice gruel. With the other ladies, she spent the rest of the day gossiping, reading romantic novels, and doing some embroidery, with time out for lunch and dinner. If it was hot, her *mui jay* would fan her and refresh her with cold towels. It was a paradise on earth, as Mama told it.

When Mama was 16, her grandmother died after an illness of only a few days. Mama happened to be the only one with her when she died; her last words voiced her concern that Mama was not yet betrothed. The body of the matriarch was placed on a bed in a room large enough to hold the entire Wong clan and their relatives. Mama remembered vividly the ceremonial rites. Sitting on the floor, sons, daughters and grandchildren attended the corpse day and night, while other relatives sat on chairs, weeping loudly and lamenting their loss. A picture of the grandmother was displayed, shrouded in white cloth — white being the color of mourning in China. The wake went on for two sleepless days and nights, and the body remained in Gim Sing Tong for a week. All that time, Mama was fearful the corpse would wake and walk around.

The body was taken to a mountainside where a temporary tomb was built. It was a year and a half before a suitable burial place was found by the geomancers. The location had to be satisfactory to *fung-shui*, the spirit of wind and water; soil and drainage had to be just right, and there must be no large trees nearby to disturb the sleeping dead when wind swept through their branches.

Twenty-one days after the death, the formal funeral ceremonies were held. Since grandmother had died in old age and in good circumstances, hers was called a "smiling death" *(sui song)*, to be celebrated with feasting and festivity. The courtyard of the compound was canopied with palm leaves to accommodate the 200 relatives who attended. The relatives brought roast pig and silk banners (poor people used wool), lauding the deceased. There were more than 200 banners, in all colors except red, 12 feet long and a

Wong Bing Woo and Tom Cherng How in Sweet Bamboo, soon after their 1898 marriage.

yard wide, decorating the courtyard. The people feasted, drank wine, and made merry *(go hing)*. Custom decreed that the death be commemorated every seventh day for seven weeks. Clad in white, the mourners prayed and feasted. On these occasions, nuns and monks were hired to chant day and night. When it was all over, the cost of grandmother's funeral and ceremonies came to $10,000.

Mama's sisters and brother married (her brother just a year before grandmother's death). The sisters married rich men — grandmother saw to that — and lived near Canton. Their wedding ceremonies were elaborate. Mama said none of the Wong girls wanted to marry because it meant leaving the family home and going to live with a strange man and his family. Yet there was never any thought of rebellion; girls were brought up knowing that some day a marriage would be arranged for them. They could only hope that the man would not be too ugly, or the mother-in-law too strict. So in the midst of the joyous wedding festivities, the center of all attention, the bride, would be frightened and red-eyed with weeping.

CHAPTER 3

Betrothal and Marriage

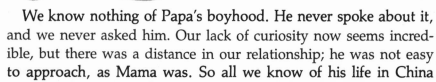

We know nothing of Papa's boyhood. He never spoke about it, and we never asked him. Our lack of curiosity now seems incredible, but there was a distance in our relationship; he was not easy to approach, as Mama was. So all we know of his life in China comes from Mama, who knew nothing of his early years.

Papa's father was a minor government official. He had eight brothers and four sisters, many of whom died young. His great grandfather had been a merchant prince who had made a fortune in tea and rice, but his sons lived indolent lives. By the time Papa's generation came along, the family fortune had dwindled. But Papa must have been bright and ambitious, judging from his later life, and he was especially eager for a good education. He took two or three classical examinations in the hope of becoming an official, but when the old examination system was abolished, Papa became a student in Canton in a school called "Thatched Hut Among Ten Thousand Trees." It was taught by Kang Yu-wei, who became the most powerful influence in Papa's life. Kang was a philosopher, poet, and political reformer who became famous in Chinese history as the leader of the Hundred Days of Reform — from June to September, 1898.

Papa was a devoted disciple of Kang and his movement to introduce Western science and technology. Kang won the support of the young Manchu Emperor Kuang-hsu, who shared his progressive ideas. They drew up edicts of reform concerning agriculture, education, economics and the military. The bold reform program lasted only 100 days. The emperor's aunt, the powerful and crafty Empress Dowager Tzu-hsi, known as Old Buddha, revoked the edicts and imprisoned the emperor in the Summer Palace. Kang fled from China. There was a reward of 100,000 taels of silver offered for his capture, dead or alive.

The Tom family strongly opposed Papa's attendance at the "Thatched Hut Among Ten Thousand Trees" and his strong ties to Kang, whom they considered a dangerous radical. Mama thought Papa studied at Kang's school for three years. During that time, he met Liang Chi-chao, Kang's leading disciple, whom Papa greatly admired. Kang's students were imbued not only with his ideas of institutional reform, but also with his theories about the Confucian classics. Papa was probably considered a "liberal" in his day as compared with his "conservative" family. His close association with Kang continued until his teacher's death in 1927. They toured the United States together seeking funds for Kang's reform program and corresponded frequently. I have donated to the UCLA Oriental Library the many letters and poems that Kang sent to Papa. They are of great historical value, and are written in Kang's unique script which can only be deciphered by scholars.

While Papa was enjoying the stimulating and exciting atmosphere of Kang's school, he received news from home that it was time for him to marry. In fact, he was told, a bride had already been chosen for him. Her name, of course, was Wong Bing Woo. Perhaps Papa's family thought that marriage would divert him from his devotion to Kang and what they considered a revolutionary program. But the news came as a blow to Papa, who was not eager to be married. However, whatever his private feelings, he was not enough of a rebel to defy the age-old tradition of arranged marriages.

The idea of matching Papa and Mama was the result of a friendship between Papa's cousin, Tom Sook Jung, a minor official in Sun

Duck district, and Mama's uncle, Wong Jo Kai (the husband of Aunt Beautiful Pearl), also a small-time bureaucrat. They were in Canton one day on official business, and afterward dropped in to see Papa at Kang's school. Uncle Jo Kai took an immediate liking to Papa and decided he was just the husband for his little niece, Frosted Porcelain, who was still not betrothed at the ripe age of 16. He was impressed by Papa's intelligence, his good looks and promising future, which he thought far outweighed the Tom family's lack of material wealth. Mama's father was not as eager to see his daughter married as were her uncle and aunt, so he left the arrangements to them. A family conference was held, and it was decided to go ahead with the match. Papa's father was invited to come to the Wong compound and was allowed a glimpse of Frosted Porcelain. Apparently, he liked what he saw.

The two young people most affected had no part in the consultations. Papa was invited to Gim Sing Tong so the Wongs could appraise him. Mama remembered passing through the courtyard one day and seeing this strange young man. She knew he must be of good standing because he wore a long gown and a round hat with a brim on it, and, she conceded, he was handsome. He must have noticed her, too. It was the first and only time they saw each other before their marriage. Mama denied she suspected anything, but strange young men did not often come visiting. Marriage was the thing she most dreaded, and she tried not to think about it. Long communications were exchanged between the two families, recounting their backgrounds for generations. Health histories were especially important to make certain there was no insanity in the ancestry. These preliminaries were detailed and time-consuming, and the formal betrothal was announced when both sides were satisfied. Papa and Mama were both 18. Papa's family sent betrothal presents of gold earrings, scrolls, cakes, tea and *bun long* (a kind of hard seed to suck on).

Aunt Beautiful Pearl and Uncle Jo Kai were eager to see a quick marriage, but Mama's father wanted to keep his daughter a little longer. As for Papa, he wasn't eager to marry; he enjoyed his life as a scholar. Two sad events gave the young couple a reprieve from the dreaded marriage. Papa's mother died a year after the betrothal, and six months later his father died. To comply with the customs of the day, the marriage did not take place for five years from the time of betrothal. For the funeral ceremonies, the Wongs sent roast pigs and cloth scrolls of every color but red, which is the color of happiness.

Mama savored those last years at home, knowing they were numbered. Finally, came *Gee Yut,* the Day of Knowing. Aunt Beautiful Pearl took Mama aside one night after dinner and gently told her that the time had come for her to be married, and that the ceremony would take place in 12 days. Mama burst into tears, and for the first time in her obedient life, she rebelled. "No, no, I won't do it," she cried over and over, though in her heart, she knew it would do no good. Years later, recalling this traumatic event to us, Mama's eyes filled with tears.

Custom required that during the 12 days before the marriage ceremony, the bride-to-be must be sequestered in her room. She was visited by women relatives and girl friends, who tried to comfort her. Instead of stemming her tears, they ended up by joining her. Meantime, dressmakers prepared her wedding wardrobe. There was a ceremonial exchange of letters between the Toms and the Wongs. First, Wong Mei Pun received a red-lacquered box containing a red envelope ten inches wide and two feet long. In it was a letter written by the head of the Tom clan which, when unfolded, was six feet long and two feet wide. It was an acknowledgment of the honor bestowed on the Toms by the choice of their son to be the husband of Wong Bing Woo. It belittled Tom Cherng How (Papa's name) and highly praised the Wong daughter. This was a ritual letter, written at great length, and it was expected by Wong Mei Pun. He had a similar letter already written on red paper with characters in gold in which he denigrated his daughter and declared her unworthy of the scion of the Tom family. This letter was placed in the red-lacquered box and delivered to the Toms. These two documents were important because they were the only record of the marriage and were placed in the archives of the House of Tom.

Next came the exchange of gifts. A procession of Tom retainers made their way to Gim Sing Tong bearing packages of delicacies, pewter canisters of expensive tea, packages of yardage goods, scrolls on which poems were written in excellent calligraphy, and a pair of gold earrings. The latter was a symbol of marriage, like a wedding ring. Two groups of musicians accompanied the procession, providing a deafening din. The whole parade was headed by two large lanterns borne on poles with the inscription of the House of Tom. The Wongs then sent their bearers, with musicians and lanterns, to the Tom home. Their gifts were more substantial, since this was to be the bride's home; they included furniture, dishes, wash basins, chamber pots, trunks of clothes, boxes of jewelry and hair ornaments. The year was 1898.

Mama's eyes brimmed with tears when she described to us her dreaded wedding day. She said she had cried continually for the 12 days since the Day of Knowing, and her eyes were red and swollen. Her servants bathed her, combed her long, black hair and pinned it up with jeweled ornaments. They had to powder and rouge her face several times to cover the ravages of tears. Her lips were tinted with red paper, not lipstick. Then her two *mui jays* helped her into her resplendent, red silk, wedding robe, edged in gold and dangling tiny bells that tinkled delicately when she moved. They put tiny slippers on her lily feet and settled an elaborate headdress carefully over her hair. Attached to the headdress was a veil of pearls that curtained her face. Aunt Beautiful Pearl came in to make a final inspection. She turned the disconsolate bride this way and that to make certain she was dressed to perfection.

The red sedan chair, in which a woman may ride but once in her lifetime, arrived in the courtyard, causing great commotion. It was quickly surrounded by the whole of the Wong clan and its retinue of servants, all gathered to bid farewell to Bing Woo. It was the end of her happy years at Gim Sing Tong as part of the Wong family; she was going to a strange home, and to a strange family whom she had never met. There was no kissing or embracing — that was not the Chinese way. It was a sad time and everyone wept, even Wong Mei Pun, as his daughter entered the sedan chair, which was fancifully carved and decorated with kingfisher feathers and borne by eight men.

A large entourage of lantern bearers, servants, and marchers accompanied the bridal chair to the Tom compound. The journey took four hours, from four in the afternoon till eight at night.

Two bands of eight players each kept up a constant din. Six girl servants were in the procession. Two of them stayed with the bride in her new home. They had been purchased for her when she was six years old for $60 each. One of these *mui jay* had been bought especially to carry the train of her wedding gown, and this duty she carried out. Also accompanying the bride were her younger brothers and sisters, who went as far as the river where the sedan chair was placed on a boat to make the crossing to Jo Tan to the Tom household. Crowds of people lined the riverbank to watch the wedding procession. Mama recalled that she had a terrible headache by this time, which was not helped by the clamor of the musicians and the weight of the headdress. She was emotionally exhausted and felt abandoned and alone despite the large entourage that accompanied her. Though she could see little from her sedan chair, she knew when she had reached her destination because the musicians let go with a final ear-splitting blast that made her head reel. The weary bearers lowered the chair to the ground outside the Tom courtyard.

Then came the dramatic moment when the groom, Papa, tapped gently on the door of the chair with his fan. As the assembled clan shouted greetings, Mama was lifted out of the chair — she said she was too weak to move — and carried on the back of a woman servant into the bridal chambers. Her face was hidden behind the veil of silk and pearls, but she got a glimpse of her new husband and saw that he was a handsome, serious-faced, young man. He wore a blue robe with red silk around his shoulders and a round mandarin hat edged with scarlet and topped with a red button.

Not until she had rested awhile and regained some composure, was Papa allowed to enter the room where she was attended by her two *mui jays*. They had been imploring her not to cry any more. He joined their plea and took off her headdress so he could see her face for the first time. Mama was never a beauty, but she was dainty and doll-like, with large eyes and fine-textured, ivory skin, and a wealth of glossy, black hair. (We have pictures of Mama and Papa soon after their marriage, but unfortunately, none taken in their younger days.) She was given a cup of tea and the little silver waterpipe she had brought from home so she could have a smoke to relax her nerves. All this time she kept her eyes averted from her husband and spoke little, but her tears had dried.

Feeling calmer, she was conducted to the family altar where she knelt with Papa and prayed to the goddess Kwan Yin. For the first time, she looked directly at him as they bowed to each other. Mama never mentioned a specific wedding ceremony, perhaps there was none. A private wedding feast was served in the bridal chamber for the young couple, followed by a banquet in the dining room with relatives and special guests. No members of the Wong family were present, for Mama was now a member of the Tom clan, even though she retained her own name. As befits a new bride, she kept her eyes downcast, did not speak, and ate hardly anything. Papa, she remembered, got half drunk, sitting at a table with his school friends. According to custom, men and women sat at separate tables. The long, exhausting, wedding day ended with Papa's friends pushing him into the nuptial chamber. The date was November 19, in the 23rd year of the reign of Emperor Kuang-hsu.

The real festivities got under way the next day. First the bride and groom, dressed in red, worshipped at the shrine of the Tom ancestors. Then the guests started arriving, several hundred of them, for the great wedding banquet in the courtyard where a special roof of palm thatch shaded the tables. The celebration went on for three days. Guests who had journeyed from afar were provided beds. They feasted day and night while several bands of musicians kept up a constant din. Mama, shielding her face modestly behind a fan, went from table to table, escorted by an older woman. Red-wrapped *lai see* was placed on a plate for the newlyweds. Papa also made the rounds of the tables. Drinking at each, he got drunk, which was expected of the groom. There were gifts galore, including gold jewelry, coins, silk and embroidered fabrics, and foodstuffs. Mama said she was extremely tired when the celebration finally ended, and the guests departed. And Papa must have had a dandy hangover!

PHOTOGRAPH OF T. LEUNG
GENERAL MANAGER OF
THE T. LEUNG HERB CO.

CONTENTS

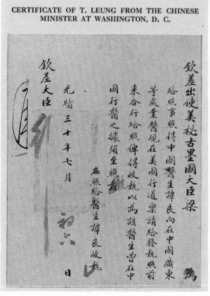

CERTIFICATE OF T. LEUNG FROM THE CHINESE MINISTER AT WASHINGTON, D. C.

Facsimile of T. Leung's Certificate from The Chinese Consul-General

Tom Leung's famous Herbal Science Booklet, published 1928.

CHAPTER 4

Papa Goes to Gold Mountain

After the wedding, Papa was eager to return to his studies in Canton at the "Thatched Hut Among Ten Thousand Trees." By that time, his beloved teacher, Kang Yu-wei, had fled from China after his brief moment of glory with the Hundred Days of Reform. Those must have been exciting times for Papa. He kept in close touch with his mentor by letter as Kang traveled from country to country seeking support for Emperor Kuang-hsu, who had been placed in confinement by Old Buddha. No doubt all the students at the school felt themselves a part of history.

Mama didn't feel abandoned by her new husband. She was delighted she could go home after staying nine days in the Tom household, as required by custom. With her husband in Canton, there was no reason for Mama to stay, since her parents-in-law were dead. Had either of them been alive, she would have had to do what new wives always did, serve them. Mama was to make the trip between Papa's home in Jo Tan and the Wong home in Yo Tan many times. Custom decreed that she be in her husband's home on all holidays to pay homage to the Tom ancestors, for special events, and whenever Papa came home from Canton. Mama said the population of Yo Tan was about 20,000, but Jo Tan was much bigger, and there was a large business district on that side of the river. Yo Tan was mostly residential, and Mama's home was about two blocks from the river. There were huge boulders along the shore, and boats had to be pulled upstream by manpower; Mama said there were many shipwrecks. This description of rocks coincides with what Jane and I were told by our host at the Gum Jook hydraulic power plant. He said the place was known as the "100 Fierce Dragons Area" because ships were wrecked on the rocks, drowning hundreds of passengers. Since the 1949 revolution, he told us, the rocks were blasted and the river "tamed." This is now called the "Happy Area." I wondered if Papa and Mama would recognize the place today.

At first when Mama returned to her own home, she was shy about seeing her old friends, fearing they would tease her about being married. She also avoided her male relatives and spent most of her time with her aunts and the older women. Apparently, Papa did not keep her informed on his scholastic activities in Canton. In his booklet, *Chinese Herbal Science*, which he published years later in Los Angeles, he described his education as revolving around the study of medicine. There is no mention of Kang, the teacher who was the greatest influence in his life. Mama indicated that Papa never studied herbal medicine until he came to this country. She knew about his intention of becoming an official, or *goon*, but when the examination was abolished, he had to turn elsewhere for a career. Biographical materials in the booklet about Papa and what we learned from Mama do not jibe. The booklet says that "for six generations past his family had been a race of physicians," while Mama told us that his father was a minor official and his great grandfather had been a merchant prince. Whoever wrote the book must have gotten his material from Papa, who may have wanted to give the impression that he had studied for years to become an herb doctor. There is a translation of a certificate purportedly from the Chinese Minister at Washington, D.C., which reads: "To all whom it may concern: This is to certify that Tom Leung is a Chinese physician of regular standing, who has been practicing medicine in the Province of Kwangtung, China; and that he is now in the United States on business connected with his profession." It is signed by Chintung Lunngsking, His Imperial Chinese Majesty's Envoy Extraordinary and Minister Plenipotentiary. The date was August 16, 1904.

If Papa had ever practiced medicine in Kwangtung, Mama knew nothing about it. Exactly how Papa acquired his knowledge of herbal medicine remains a mystery. Obviously, Papa hired someone to write the booklet, published in 1928, but the author is unknown.

With Kang out of the country, and with no prospects of becoming a government official, Papa's career seemed to be at a dead-end even before it started. He enjoyed his studies, but he knew his life as a student could not continue forever. He was an ambitious young man, so he was delighted when he received an invitation from E Bok Foo, a cousin (his father's brother's son), to come to Gold Mountain. E Bok Foo, whose name was Tom Foo Yuen, had established an herb company in Los Angeles several years previously. He wanted to visit China and needed a replacement. He considered Papa the most promising of the young men in the Tom clan. To Papa's adventurous spirit, this was an opportunity he could not resist. He was eager to see the strange, new country. Mama was seven months pregnant and had no desire to leave China, but she was perfectly willing that Papa should go.

There were several farewell parties at the Tom and Wong homes, with much eating and drinking. Papa was given gifts, such as dried shark fins, dried and canned sea food, dried plums, dried peaches, and other foodstuffs which would not be available in America. Although his stay was to be temporary, he took six or seven trunks filled with books, clothes, medicines, and all the gifts. There was no kissing or embracing when he said goodbye to Mama. He was apparently more sentimental than Mama, because he asked her to give him something of hers to take with him. "I have nothing," she replied. So he took her right hand and removed a gold ring she had worn since she was a child. He said he would not be gone for long, but urged her to write him often. He had given her a crystal seal with her name engraved on it to use on the envelopes enclosing her letters to him. (At the time

Mama gave us this information, she still had the seal.) He also gave her a supply of writing brushes and paper. Mama claimed she didn't mind his leaving, but she probably had some qualms, even though she had no conception how far away Gold Mountain was.

Papa made his older brother Bok Foo (not to be confused with E Bok Foo) promise to cable him when Mama gave birth. It took half a day to get from Gum Jook to Canton by boat, and another day to get to Hong Kong where Papa embarked for America by steamer. He was accompanied to Hong Kong by a half dozen brothers and cousins. It was June or July, 1899, when Papa arrived in this country. His first destination was probably San Francisco, and from there he went to Los Angeles. We have no idea under what type of visa papers he was admitted, or how he was allowed to stay permanently in this country. He subsequently made two trips to China, but apparently he had no problems with immigration. Unfortunately, we have no first-hand information from him as to his impressions of America. E Bok Foo's business, called the Foo and Wing Herb Company, was located in a large Victorian house at 903 S. Olive Street in a quiet residential neighborhood (now the heart of downtown Los Angeles). At first Papa worked as a cashier for the company, but he was a quick learner, and under E Bok Foo's tutelage, was soon prescribing and dispensing herbs. He had brought from China a large library of herb books, and he studied them constantly.

How E Bok Foo learned herbal medicine is another mystery. Although he spoke little, if any, English, he had managed to build up quite a clientele. He always wore Chinese robes and a round Mandarin hat. His right-hand man was named Hallowell, a quiet, pleasant bachelor who served as secretary, interpreter (though he didn't speak Chinese), errand boy and general factotum for E Bok Foo, to whom he was devoted.

Unlike E Bok Foo, Papa was determined to learn English so he could communicate with the patients. He hired Paul Howard, a young man whose family operated a flower nursery across the street, to teach him. (Howard later became one of the leading horticulturists in Los Angeles.) A notebook of that period shows Papa's handwriting was very clear and legible. Papa never learned to speak fluently, however, and about the only writing he did was to sign his name. He understood English much better than he spoke it and never seemed to have trouble understanding his patients.

At this time, Papa took the name Tom Leung, perhaps because he thought it would be easier for Americans to pronounce than Tom Cherng How, the name his family and friends called him, or Tom Gee Lin, his childhood name.

Tom Leung (left) studying English with Paul Howard.

Papa wrote to Mama once or twice a month. He said he liked America, particularly the conveniences such as hot and cold running water, wide paved streets, street cars, and horse-drawn carriages. However, he didn't care for American food, and he missed having servants. Sometimes he wrote poems to her saying that he missed her. The letters were written on beautiful, flower-decorated stationery in Papa's exceptionally fine calligraphy. He sent snapshots of Los Angeles and an occasional draft for $100 in Chinese money. Mama said she didn't keep any of the letters because "there were too many of them." She wrote him, using the crystal seal, but unfortunately, none of these letters were preserved.

Mama had been staying in the Wong household after Papa's departure, but during the month before the baby was expected, she went to Papa's home. It would have been a grievous breach of custom had the child been born elsewhere. The baby, a boy, was born in September, 1899, and was named Tom Jo Herng. Mama was always extremely proud of her first-born, and, from her telling, he was somewhat of a genius. Papa was notified by cable, which at that time cost $120 in Chinese money. He sent his new son some gold coins and some flowered cotton and silk materials. After a proper interval, Mama took her baby across the river to her family home. He was so bright, she said, that he was taught to read when he was only a year old. He could repeat half of the first primer when his *mui jay* read to him aloud. He was unselfish and never squabbled with the other children. *"Um sai jang* (we needn't quarrel)," she quoted him as saying. He seemed mature far beyond his age.

Though he was a tall, handsome child, he was not physically strong. When he was only 18 months old, he was suddenly stricken ill with what was probably pneumonia. Mama hurriedly took him to the Tom home. Had he died in her family home, it would have indicated that she was to blame for his death. Tom Jo Herng died the next day; his last words were "I'm already asleep." Mama said a nurse overheard him say a few days before he died, *"Bok bok yim yim yue joe yut cherng* (even evil deeds must be experienced once)." She felt this incident showed his unusual intelligence. Mama may have attributed more than his due to her dead son, but this must have been a most traumatic experience for her, with Papa in a far-away country. Tears came to her eyes whenever she mentioned her beloved first-born. Tom Jo Herng was buried with his father's ancestors. News of his death must have been a blow to Papa, who never got to see his son. No pictures were ever taken of the child because of a superstition that a baby should not be photographed before he became a toddler of three or four; it was feared that a picture would "draw the spirit out of the child."

(An interesting incident concerning the dead son occurred years later after our sister Lillie's marriage in September, 1925. Papa's older brother wrote that one of his sons had been ill since the marriage. He blamed the illness on the fact that the dead son had not married before Lillie. According to Chinese custom, siblings must marry according to age, the oldest first. Papa's brother got a "girl ghost" of a baby, who had died in another province, to marry the dead Tom Jo Herng. There was a marriage feast, tea drinking ceremony, and exchange of gifts. Subsequently, the sick son recovered. Papa was billed for the "marriage," and he sent $120 to his brother. Whether our parents really believed this superstition is unknown. Probably Papa didn't, but Mama related the incident very seriously.)

Papa, by this time, had become quite accustomed to American life and its conveniences. E Bok Foo had gone on his vacation, and Papa was handling the herb business. He continued his study of the herb books, as well as the lessons in English, and was progressing well. When he heard of the baby's death, he decided he wanted to bring Mama to this country as soon as E Bok Foo returned. The two men decided to go into business together; E Bok Foo was president, and Papa was vice-president of the Foo and Wing Herb Company.

GOODBYE TO SWEET BAMBOO

CHAPTER 5

Goodbye to Sweet Bamboo

Papa returned to China in December, 1901. He had written Mama about his plans to bring her back with him to America, but she was reluctant. She didn't want to leave China. Her father had died that January after an illness. He had just taken a fifth concubine six months before, a girl of 18, younger than Mama. Aunt Beautiful Pearl urged Mama to go to America since she now had no parents and no parents-in-law. Papa painted glowing pictures of life in Gold Mountain — he missed the flush toilets and the gas lights there. He told her she should *tai dee sai yun* (see the Western people). They would return in two or three years after he had made some money, he said. But Mama didn't have his curiosity and adventurous spirit and was frightened at the idea of leaving her home and family. This is hardly surprising since she had never been further away than the Tom home.

Meantime, Papa spent much time writing letters. He kept up a continuous correspondence with Kang Yu-wei, who was then in India. Papa's older brother disapproved of this correspondence. "If you don't care about yourself, at least you should think of your family and especially your wife," he said. Kang was in deep disfavor because of his continuing efforts to secure the release of the imprisoned Emperor Kuang-hsu, and his followers in China were also in danger. Mama said she did not dare to venture outside the Tom compound. Papa, however, ignored his brother's warnings; his loyalty to Kang was stronger than ever. He also wrote letters to his teacher, Paul Howard, and to Hallowell. There is a notebook with copies of a few of these letters. The first one, to Howard, read in part:

> After a long voyage from San Francisco to Hong Kong, I have at last reached my old home. My wife and family are all well. Although I enjoyed living in America very much, I am glad to get back to my home and family whom I have not seen for over three years. The voyage from America was extremely pleasant because we had a very calm sea. I arrived in Hong Kong on the 15th of Dec. Several of my friends met me at the steamer. After leaving S.F. our first stop was at Honolulu. There was nothing of much interest to me there. Our next one was Yokohoma. We stopped for two days. I spent my time in travelling around the city. Are you still at school and what class and grade are you? Well I will close hoping to hear from you very soon and a good long letter.

It was signed, "Your affectionate pupil, Tom Leung."

Finding these letters was a surprise because they were so well written in words we had never heard him use. Howard replied, asking for "a full description of one of your Chinese villages and some of the customs in them. Do most of the villages have streams or rivers running through them?" Howard asked for pictures, especially of the interiors of houses and about the Chinese mode of travel by land. Papa's answer to this was disappointing. He wrote merely that "The village I live in is medium size. I think the population is about ten thousand." He did promise to send some pictures.

The letter to Hallowell read in part: "I am glad to get back with my family again and my wife and other relatives were very much pleased to have me return. I did not get seasick on the water, and felt quite well during the whole voyage. Many Chinese came on the steamer, but most of them came second class and of course I did not associate with them . . . I like America and hope sometime to visit your country again . . ." This letter revealed Papa's class consciousness (in not associating with second class passengers), a trait that was passed on to us as children. Hallowell's reply stated that "How Wing is learning English quite fast and speaks very well now," referring to E Bok Foo's second son, whom we called E Gow (second cousin), and who later married E Sow (second cousin's wife). Hallowell also told Papa that "Some American friends have been inquiring about you and asking if you intend to return to America."

Not until April, 1902, did Papa finally persuade Mama to go with him to Gold Mountain. She went only with the promise that they would soon return. Had she known she would never again see her homeland and family, I doubt she would have gone. Even though Papa liked America, he also intended to return as soon as he had made enough money to build a home in China. Mama had her *mui jay* pack just her clothes and a few personal items, such as her black and red lacquer bed pillow (which she later gave up for the much more comfortable American pillows) and her miniature, gold lacquer dressing table. This consisted of a folding mirror with a couple of drawers beneath to hold her large ivory comb and hairpins. This article was placed on top of a table, and Mama would sit in front of it to comb her hair. She used it every day until she became bedridden towards the end of her life. In China she never had to comb her own hair; her *mui jay* did it. Leaving her *mui jay* was as sad and wrenching for Mama as leaving her family. The servant girl was only a few years older than Mama and had been purchased for her when Mama was a child; they were like sisters. Another reason Mama dreaded leaving home was that she was pregnant again, and she feared giving birth in a strange country where she knew no one.

In order to facilitate Mama's entrance into this country as his wife, Papa took her to an American minister in Canton and had a marriage ceremony performed. Thus he had a marriage certificate to present to immigration officials. The certificate read: "This is to certify that Mr. Tom Leung and Miss Wong Ping Foo [sic] were this day joined by me in Christian marriage as man and wife, in the Preston Memorial Chapel, Kuk Fau, Canton, China." It was dated February 20, 1902, and signed by Oscar F. Wisner, Ordained minister, Presbyterian Church of the United States of America. Two witnesses, John M. Swan and Charles E. Patton, signed the certificate. Papa had a passport which the Howards had helped him obtain.

Finally, after long and tearful farewells, Papa and Mama made the journey to Canton and then to Hong Kong, where they boarded a ship called something like the "Galick," according to Mama, and sailed for America. They traveled first class — $500 Hong Kong money each. The voyage took 28 days. Mama stayed in their stateroom practically the entire time; her bound feet made it difficult for her to get around, and she was self-conscious about them as well as about her pregnancy. She had her first taste of American food (meals were eaten in their stateroom) and did not like it. She thought it had a bad odor. The one thing she did enjoy was iced watermelon. She had never had ice in China. After the first few days, Papa ordered Chinese food.

All day long Mama read the story books she had brought from China. During the very few appearances she made on deck, Mama said the passengers she met were nice to her. Although they could not communicate, these strangers smiled and were friendly when Papa introduced her. The only Caucasians that she had seen in China were missionaries, and she had no contact with them. Appearing with Papa in public was in itself a whole new way of life for Mama. In those days in China, Mama said, a wife never went out with her husband lest she be laughed at and teased.

Papa, on the other hand, enjoyed the trip. He conversed with the Americans on board using the English he had learned on his first sojourn to the States. He also did a lot of reading. He had brought books on history, biography, and the treatises of medicine. Also included in his luggage were pictures, scrolls, and a pair of bamboo plaques from his home. These now hang in my home in Topanga. Roughly translated, one reads: "Wind and moon meet those we used to know. (Old friends.)"

At last the ship arrived in San Francisco. Papa and Mama were admitted with no trouble from immigration officials and with no detainment at Angel Island or any similar place. This was fortunate, since Mama, fragile as she was and used to being waited on hand and foot, could not have withstood such hardship. Papa had arranged for relatives of the same surname (Tom) to meet them at the boat and to host them for four or five days. The strange new country was bewildering to Mama. Suddenly, she was surrounded everywhere by *bok gway* (white ghosts). She had never seen a wooden house (Chinese houses were built of stone) and was afraid they would fall down. She found the chicken and meat tasteless and thought American clothes ugly and shapeless. In addition, having to get along without the ministrations of her *mui jay* was difficult. A deep, penetrating homesickness for China set in, a feeling that stayed with her for the rest of her life, to a greater or lesser degree.

The trip to Los Angeles was made by train; it was the first time Mama had seen a railroad train. When she saw the redcaps with baggage dollies, she asked Papa, "How can a person ride in them?" fearing she would be expected to. Her fears were allayed when she was shown to their comfortable compartment. Accompanying them was a woman member of the Tom family named Bot Sum. Papa had arranged for her to stay with them in Los Angeles until Mama adjusted to her new life. Meeting them at the station in Los Angeles with a horse-driven buggy were E Gow (Tom How Wing, son of Tom Foo Yuen) and Mr. and Mrs. George Lem (the future grandparents of Richard Lem, who would marry Lillie's daughter, Patty). The Lems were pioneers in the Chinese community and became lifelong friends of our family. They were active in their church and owners of a restaurant that had a city-wide reputation for excellent Chinese food. Mama enjoyed the buggy ride — it reminded her of rickshas — that took her to her first home in Gold Mountain, 903 S. Olive Street. It was May, 1902.

CHAPTER 6

Ninth and Olive

E Bok Foo was busy with many patients, and it was some time before he could greet the new arrivals with his wife, E Bok Mo, whom he had brought back with him on his vacation in China. She was a handsome, pleasant woman who lived as though she were still in China, with no contact whatever with the Western world. She had tiny, bound feet and, like her husband, wore only Chinese clothes. Unhappy in this country, she returned to China in a few years.

Papa and Mama were given the "red room" *(hoong fong)*, a second floor living room with a red carpet which gave it its name, and a bedroom beyond. Mama spent most of her time in this *hoong fong*. She found the two-story Victorian home cramped after the large family compounds she was accustomed to. After the large retinue of servants she had in China, having now just a cook, named Gee Sook, was a hardship for her. Mama was probably also somewhat intimidated by E Bok Foo and his eccentric habits. He had to have his food cooked in a special way and rose at dawn every day to exercise in the backyard. The backyard was

The first family home in Los Angeles, 903 South Olive.

large, with a guest house and a storage building for herbs. There was only a small patch of lawn in front of the corner house, which faced on both Olive and Ninth streets — then a quiet and residential area. Downstairs was an entrance hall and the big parlor where the patients waited to see the doctors and to get their herbs. A pot belly stove made the room the only comfortable one in the winter. There were two dining rooms, one for men and the other for women, Chinese-style. A big wood range dominated the kitchen, which Gee Sook did not keep overly clean. All day long herbs were cooked on the stove for those patients who chose to take a dose of medicine before going home. There was a tin sink and counter and a round table covered with white oilcloth where Gee Sook ate his meals. The table was grimy and so was the wood floor, and Gee Sook let grease accumulate on the sink and counter. He was a large, quiet-spoken man and a good cook, who worked uncomplainingly from morning till night, when he went home to his room in Chinatown. He spoke no English and wore dark, padded Chinese clothes no matter how hot the weather. Every afternoon he took a big straw basket and boarded the streetcar for Chinatown to shop for the family dinner.

Homesick as she was, Mama delighted in the flush toilets and the water that flowed whenever she turned on the faucets. But she found it strange to sleep on a bed without a mosquito netting, and the mattress was so soft that she had Papa get a board to place beneath it. She used her Chinese pillow, but during the day hid it under an American pillow for fear it would be laughed at. She did not often eat American food, but her favorite dishes were oysters, and ham and eggs. She liked her bread steamed so it would be spongy like Chinese bread. Her favorite fruits were grapes, tart apples, and persimmons. Later on, she developed a liking for apple pie, bread pudding (which she learned to make, and all agreed it was delicious), custard, and English cookies. She never ate ice cream, saying it was too cold. Papa's favorite food was a big, juicy steak. Neither of them ever used butter, drank fresh milk, or ate cheese, which they considered an abomination. Mama would shudder at the mention of *cho* (smelly) cheese, as she called it.

For Mama, the adjustment to a strange country and a new home must have been traumatic. The household itself was a whole new world. In addition to Hallowell, there was a receptionist named Miss Akers, a small, greying woman. Her duty was to greet the patients and give each a number by which his or her treatment was subsequently identified. The patients would wait in the parlor until E Bok Foo summoned them in turn, ringing a bell. The office was upstairs, furnished with two, big, mahogany desks, one for E Bok Foo and the other for Papa. Both men wore long, silk, Chinese gowns and brocaded vests. At that time, Papa still had his queue, which he often hid by rolling it up under his round hat. The desks were fitted with glass panels in the middle with the patient on one side and the doctor on the other. There was room beneath the glass for a silk cushion on which the patient rested his hand for pulse-taking, an integral part of Chinese medicine. It was believed that by feeling the pulse, a great deal could be learned about the condition of the body. E Bok Foo would write a prescription with a Chinese brush on a piece of white paper, and Papa would review it and feel the patient's pulse. Sometimes, he would change a part of the prescription, which would result in an argument. (This must have been unsettling to the patient, especially since the two men spoke in Chinese to each other.) E Bok Foo was the senior partner in the firm and considered himself in charge, but Papa soon had a following of his own. Papa was young, spoke more English, and developed a rapport with the patients.

The druggist, who at that time was Jo Lop Way, made up the prescriptions. His domain was the herb room in which there were banks of drawers, each holding a species of herb. Papa's book "Chinese Herbal Science" says there were 3000 species of herbs in use, with 10 to 18 varieties in each prescription. The herbs were grown in the mountains and valleys of China and imported to this country. They were comprised of substances such as roots, barks, flowers, leaves and berries. The druggist usually made up a week's supply of the medicines. Using a pie pan for each dose, he would very carefully follow the prescription, choosing the right herb from the drawers. Occasionally, he had to weigh an herb, but usually he could pick up just the right amount. If a patient wanted to take a dose at the office, Jo Lop Way would add several cups of water to the contents of one pie pan and boil it until there was one cup of brew. The other doses would be carefully put into separate paper bags, neatly folded and wrapped for the patient to take home. Often there were several patients sitting at the big table in the men's dining room, sipping the bitter brew which was served with a dish of raisins to sweeten the taste. (Because of this association with the bitter tea, no one in our family likes raisins.) The average cost of the herbs was $10 a week.

A few days after Mama arrived in Los Angeles, Mrs. Lem brought Mrs. Emma Findlay to see her. The Lems were active members of the Congregational Church, which Mrs. Findlay also attended. She made it her career to welcome Chinese women to Los Angeles and was well-known and loved for decades in the Chinese community. A lovely, sweet-faced woman, she was truly Christian and unselfish. Until her death in her 80's, she brought Mama a Christmas gift every year, and Mama always had something for her in return. She never tried to "convert" her Chinese friends, but if they were interested in attending church, she would gladly take them. Papa and Mama had no such interest; Papa followed Confucianism, which is not a religion, but a philosophy. Mrs. Findlay gave Mama some lessons in English, teaching her from a primer for $5 a month. She came three times a week, riding her bicycle. The textbook was elementary, with such phrases as "I see mama. I see papa." The lessons were a trial for Mama — she thought that English was much more difficult to learn than Chinese. She mastered a few commonly used words and learned to write "Mrs. T. Leung" laboriously. Though she never did speak the language well, she eventually did understand much of what was said. Papa resumed his lessons with Paul Howard, but they stopped after a while when both became too busy. Papa learned just enough to communicate with the patients. He and Mama spoke only Chinese to each other, which was natural. Occasionally Papa brought some patients to the *hoong fong* to meet Mama. About all she could do to communicate with them was to smile graciously and offer them tea. There was always a pot of tea kept hot in a cotton-padded straw basket. Mama especially remembered a lawyer and his wife, and a German woman, Mrs. Bok. Several patients invited Papa and Mama to see the sights with them and to go to dinner, but Mama felt too shy and self-conscious to accept, especially because she was pregnant.

CHAPTER 7

Lillie's Birth

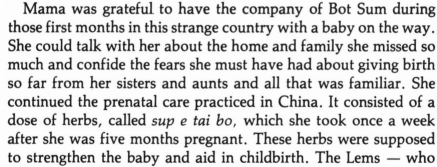

Mama was grateful to have the company of Bot Sum during those first months in this strange country with a baby on the way. She could talk with her about the home and family she missed so much and confide the fears she must have had about giving birth so far from her sisters and aunts and all that was familiar. She continued the prenatal care practiced in China. It consisted of a dose of herbs, called *sup e tai bo*, which she took once a week after she was five months pregnant. These herbs were supposed to strengthen the baby and aid in childbirth. The Lems — who also were to have a large family — brought a Mrs. Mueller, a midwife, to meet Mama. A stocky, muscular woman who spoke with a heavy German accent, Mrs. Mueller had been introduced to the Chinese community by Mrs. Findlay. She was midwife to all the Chinese women in Los Angeles, who of course would never have consented going to the hospital for delivery. One of her duties was to buy the baby's layette, since the mother-to-be would find this impossible to do. Mrs. Mueller very soon became indispensable to the busy household.

In addition to the herbs, Mama also followed her homeland custom of eating black sesame seed pudding *(gee mah woo)* during the last months of her pregnancies. She believed this took the "poison" out of the unborn child and eased childbirth. After delivery, she drank vinegar wine, which was supposed to clear out waste. Her post-partum diet also included chicken broth with wine, eggs and rice. This regime seemed to agree with her. Though she was tiny and looked frail, no one in the house heard even a whimper from her during her eight labors. There were never any complications. Mama usually stayed in bed for two weeks and then was up and about as usual. Mrs. Mueller was called as soon as labor began. Wearing a white uniform, she would scurry around boiling water. Most of the time, the babies were born at night. The next morning there would be a new baby, and Mama's room would have what we children called the "new baby smell," a combination of talcum powder, fresh baby clothes, and Mama's chicken wine. Mrs. Mueller charged $15, but Papa always paid her $20, to her delight.

Mama brought with her from China some beliefs — or superstitions — about pregnancy and childbirth. She never admitted to believing them, but she talked about them seriously. For example, it was believed that if a pregnant woman dreams of red flowers she will have a girl; if she dreams of white flowers, she will have a boy. Mama recalled that her aunt cut out a dragon of red paper and placed it under the bed of a pregnant woman in the Wong household. When the infant was born, it bore a red mark in the shape of a dragon on one of its arms. Mama said that a woman who ate a lot of egg whites would bear a child with fair skin. Since she did not like egg whites, all of us children have dark skins like Papa's, instead of fair skin like hers.

She made a practice of reading good books during pregnancy because of her firm belief that prenatal influence could affect a baby's character. She recalled that when she was carrying William, she read a story about a temple on a rugged mountain which could only be reached by a daring young man. That, she believed, explained why William was such an adventurous baby, climbing out of his crib before he was a year old to help himself to some candy. When she was pregnant with me, she went to

Chinatown and made a speech, a most unusual act for a Chinese woman. That is why I turned out to be aggressive and unmanageable, she believed.

On the evening of September 7, 1902, Mama had dinner with Bot Sum in the *hoong fong*. Soon after, Mama went into labor, and at 10 p.m. Lillie was born. Lillie weighed 10 pounds and was chubby, with a very flat face and nose. A newspaper account of her month-old banquet mentioned her little flat nose. E Bok Foo used a turtle shell to tell fortunes, and he had predicted that the baby would be a boy. When he heard that it was a girl, he was so angry that his vaunted prediction was wrong, that he went to his room and slammed the door. Papa was also disappointed in not having a boy because he had never seen his first-born son.

Mama didn't nurse her children. We were all brought up on evaporated condensed milk (Eagle brand), which Mama called "condensum" and which was probably recommended by Mrs. Mueller. Bot Sum took care of Lillie, whose Chinese name was Mook Lan, after Mama's favorite heroine. When Lillie was a month old, all her hair was cut off, and a special ceremony was held in the dining room at 903 S. Olive just before noon. It was a prayer to the gods of China for the newborn. Papa and Mama stood by silently, their hands tucked into their sleeves, as the cook, Gee Sook, intoned a prayer for long life and happiness for the infant, who was held by Jo Lop Way, the druggist. All present kowtowed to the gods in the sky. This ceremony was held only for Lillie. Papa decided it was unnecessary for babies born in America. However, the custom of giving red eggs, ginger and pork to friends and relatives was always carried out. Also, when an infant reached its first moon, the month-old banquet was given. Lillie's banquet was held in Chinatown. There were 10 tables (100 guests) including relatives, friends, and some patients. She received many gifts, notably gold bracelets and necklaces. The festive event was written up in the local press, but regrettably, no clippings were kept.

After Lillie's birth, there was another memorable occasion for Mama. She unbound her feet. Several times a day she soaked her feet in herbs. Although they were remained stunted, it must have been a great relief to remove the cloths that had bound them tightly for so many years. She now wore white socks and soft Chinese slippers. She said she had to learn to walk all over again. Papa was happy about the unbinding because he felt the custom abhorrent, a belief he picked up in Kang Yu-wei's school. Kang was also very much opposed to the queue.

CHAPTER 8

Mama, the Women's Liberationist

With Bot Sum to look after Lillie, and with her feet unbound, Mama began a more active life. Papa had high-button shoes custom-made for her from New York. They cost $5 a pair, and Papa had several pairs made so Mama wouldn't have to subject herself to frequent measurings by the shoe salesman. The shoes were never comfortable, however, and Mama wore them only when she went out. Her last pair, which cost $20, lasted 10 years. After she got her first pair of American shoes, she went with Mrs. Findlay to buy some American clothes. They went to Hamburgers, later called the May Co., at Eighth and Broadway, just a few blocks from 903 S. Olive. Her first dress was of plain, light blue silk, with the waist and skirt separate. It had a high neck, long sleeves, and a lace collar. Mrs. Findlay helped her buy underwear as well as a $25 hat, ostrich feathers extra. Mama hated the hat — it made her head ache. She liked the clothes but didn't know how to put them on. Papa was pleased with the new wardrobe; it delighted him to see her in American clothes. Bot Sum, who had bought a black dress on a prior shopping trip, was resentful because Mama's dress was prettier than hers. Mama never bought everyday, American dresses to wear at home because she never felt comfortable in anything but *tong chong* (Chinese clothes). The pretty silk dress was worn only when she went out, because she would have felt conspicuous wearing *tong chong*. Papa bought her jewels and furs for which she had little use. She did like the one-karat diamond earrings he gave her — perhaps because she was accustomed to wearing earrings since her ears were pierced as a child.

Mrs. Findlay also taught Mama how to put up her hair in a pompadour style, drawing it high over the forehead over a roll of artificial hair called a "rat." She wore bangs and a black, satin, rosette bow on one side of her hairdo. She combed her hair in this style for years until she finally eliminated the "rat" and the bow. On her dressing table was the gold lacquer box with the folding mirror and the drawers for her combs which she had brought from China. She always sat in front of this to do her hair each morning.

Perhaps the reason Papa liked to see Mama in American dresses was because he himself adjusted quickly to American attire. When he first returned to America with Mama, he wore Chinese robes but soon bought himself American suits. While seeing patients, however, he continued for years to wear Chinese clothes, thinking, perhaps, that it would enhance his image as an Oriental herbalist. He had his suits custom-made by the finest tailors, paying about $200 for them, an extravagant amount in those days. His shirts were of white Chinese silk, made to his order, and he soon accumulated a large collection of expensive ties. In the summer he wore immaculate, white flannels and dark coats. He never went out — even for a short walk — without a hat, a fedora in winter and a Panama in summer. He carried a gold-headed walking stick (I still have the head) — not because he needed it, but because he considered it stylish. His tie-pin was a cluster of three large pearls. Diamonds were his favorite gem, and he wore a one or two karat diamond ring. In the early years, he had a gold watch in his upper coat pocket; from the watch chain dangled a gold heart inscribed with Chinese characters. His cuff links were of gold. He always looked immaculate and well-groomed and was perhaps the best-dressed Chinese gentleman in Los Angeles. Even around the house, he maintained his good grooming; he didn't change into comfortable, old clothes after work or on weekends.

When Papa first started wearing Western clothes, there was the problem of his queue. Mama said he solved this by buying a wig which he wore over it. Although he felt as strongly about the queue as his teacher Kang, he did not have it cut off until shortly before Taft (our parents' first American-born son) was born in 1909. Papa was afraid to go to the barber shop for fear he would be ridiculed. Finally, Mama urged him to go to Chinatown to the Chinese barber. When his hated queue was gone, he was as happy as Mama when she unbound her feet. "My whole head feels light," he said. He got rid of the wig. Mama said she saved the queue.

When Lillie was a few months old, Mama resumed her English lessons with Mrs. Findlay, a half hour three times a week. She still found the language very difficult and gave up after a while. She was homesick and wanted to return to China, but Papa said he must make more money first. She had promised Aunt Beautiful Pearl and her other relatives that she would not stay long in Gold Mountain; she longed for the sights and sounds of Sweet Bamboo. Papa, however, was enjoying his life here. He was doing well in the herb business and perhaps saw no career for himself in China. There must have been much correspondence with their families in China, but we have no letters from the earliest years.

Papa enjoyed going places around Los Angeles and persuaded Mama to go with him after Lillie was born. One of his favorites was Mt. Lowe in the San Gabriel mountains, north of Pasadena. It boasted of having "the greatest mountain trolley trip in the world." The Alpine Railway twisted and turned for miles up the mountains. Mama went to Mt. Lowe three times — once they took Mrs. Findlay. Mama said other women on the trolley would shut their eyes as it climbed toward the clouds, but she liked the scenery and the good air. At the end of the line there was a tavern where they rested and had refreshments. When friends came from China, Papa took them to Mt. Lowe. The popular resort closed in

1936, a victim of the Depression years.

Once Papa took Mama to the Tournament of Roses. They went by horse and buggy, starting at 6 a.m. because it took three hours to get there. They stood up along the parade route. Mama said she got very tired, but Papa liked parades. He also took her to the circus, which she found dirty and smelly. They sat in the front row, and Mama feared the horses would get out of the ring and run over her. They also went to a rodeo, which, strangely enough, Mama enjoyed — she liked to watch the cowboys — but Papa didn't, because he thought it was dangerous. Mama remembered going to the Orange Show in San Bernardino, but she didn't accompany Papa to the county fair in Pomona because there was too much walking. On all these adventures, Mama wore her American clothes. One can imagine her at the circus in her silk dress and hat with the ostrich feather. Papa always held her arm when escorting her. In China, it had been considered unseemly if she appeared in public with her husband. Even in this country some Chinese husbands still were reluctant to escort their wives in public style. Though she never said so, Mama seemed to enjoy Papa's attentiveness.

Mrs. Findlay arranged church picnics at Lincoln Park for the Chinese women and children. Mama went to a few of these but didn't particularly enjoy them. Lillie went with her new nurse, Mrs. Elva Brooker, recommended by American friends. Bot Sum had returned to San Francisco when Lillie was a year old. Mrs. Brooker worked from 6 a.m. to 6 p.m. for $30 a month. She brought Mama her wash basin in the morning, Chinese style. When Mama went out, Mrs. Brooker helped her dress in her American clothes. She even showed Papa how to tie his ties. She stayed with the family for three years and was such a good friend that Lillie was given the name Elva as her second name. Many years later, Mrs. Brooker's daughter, Wilma, came to work for Papa as his secretary.

Another old-time friend was Frank Frank, a neighborhood boy whom Papa met during his first visit to America. Frank Frank (we always marveled at his name) remembered when Papa disappeared and returned later with a wife. Frank and the other neighborhood boys were greatly impressed by Papa's fireworks displays on July 4. The boys would gather around in front of "903" and take turns setting off the fireworks. Papa spent as much as $50 on a variety of them, including Roman candles and a six-foot skyrocket that had to be braced alongside a ladder. (Fireworks were legal in those days). The climax of the celebration was setting off a 50-foot long string of Chinese firecrackers, the explosions erupting for ten minutes. The whole neighborhood watched the "Chinaman" celebrate. He did this every July 4 for years, not out of patriotism, but because he loved the spectacle. Perhaps the fireworks reminded him of China. The holiday was an excuse for a big display.

Frank was a dedicated stamp collector and received many Chinese stamps from Papa. He maintained his friendship with our family until his death in 1980. Every two weeks, on a Saturday afternoon, he would visit us, always bringing a gift of the choicest candy. On Easter his gift was a large chocolate Easter egg, very rich, which would last for weeks. He made friends with several other Chinese families also, and had a little black book in which he kept dates of birthdays, graduations, weddings, deaths and miscellaneous data. It was said that Frank Frank knew more about people than they knew themselves; he had a lifelong and genuine interest in the Chinese community. A bachelor, he lived with his mother, and the two would often go fishing, taking their poles and baskets and riding to the beach on the Red Cars, which were running at that time. Although he had a good job at the Security First National Bank, Frank never owned a car.

A memorable event for Mama in 1904 was a visit by her younger brother Wong Che Tat, who was sent here by the Chinese government as representative to the World's Fair in St. Louis. When he came to Los Angeles, he made speeches in Chinatown. Mama herself went to the platform once, though she was several months pregnant with me. She said she spoke for half an hour on the subject of women in China. She said Chinese women should be taught to read and write so they would not be dominated by men and husbands should not be allowed to have concubines. It was difficult to imagine our gentle mother haranguing from the soapbox, probably one of the first Chinese women liberationists. As she recalled it, she herself seemed

amazed, but proud, of her daring. *"Um pa cho* (not ashamed),"
she said. Asked if she had prepared her speech, she said, "Why
should I? It was all in my stomach. I talked till I was red in the
face." That was Mama's one and only public speech, though she
said she argued with Papa and his friends on the subject of concubines. They claimed there were too many women in China, and
therefore, a man had to have more than one woman; that was the
only way women could be supported and protected. On the subject of education for women, Papa totally agreed with her.

When her brother returned to China, Mama wanted to go with
him, but he agreed with Papa that she should stay here. Mama
wanted the companionship of her woman relatives and servants
to take care of her and Lillie.

CHAPTER 9

Intrigue at Olive Street

Papa never wavered in his devotion to the cause of Kang Yu-wei, who was wandering from country to country after his exile from China. Kang attempted, unsuccessfully, to enlist the aid of foreign governments to obtain the release of the Emperor Kuang-hsu, who was still held prisoner by Old Buddha. In overseas Chinese communities, he organized a reform movement variously called "Society to Protect the Emperor," "Society for Constitutional Government," or "Empire Reform Society." Papa, of course, was active in this movement. One way in which he supported it was to take students from China, followers of Kang, into his home, where they lived free of charge. There was a small house in the backyard at 903 S. Olive where they lived, one or two at a time, while they attended local colleges.

In 1903, Liang Chi-chao, whom Papa had met at Kang's school, and who was now considered the most prominent reformer after Kang Yu-wei, visited Los Angeles. Liang was vice president of the Empire Reform Society and was in this country to visit various chapters. His arrival was considered important

Tom Leung (standing) with the famed Kang Yu-wei, 1905.

enough to be noted in the *Los Angeles Times*, which stated that Liang was met at the railroad station by "local dignitaries and 20 carriages of prominent Chinese in flowered robes." The *Times* article was quoted in the book *Homer Lea, Sun Yat-Sen and the Chinese Revolution* by Eugene Anschel. Papa was surely among the Chinese who welcomed Liang. Anschel's book also noted that "A lavish banquet was given by a Dr. Tom Leung, whose name, incidentally, would also reappear in the story of Homer Lea. Guests of the banquet included prominent Chinese from Los Angeles, San Francisco and Sacramento. The only non-Chinese present was Homer Lea."

The mention of Papa indicates his leadership in the reform movement in Los Angeles. Lea was a soldier of fortune who claimed to be general of the Chinese Imperial Reform Army and was active in the reform movement. However, he was described as an opportunist, always out for his own interests. Later on, when Kang and Sun Yat-sen became rivals and the latter was winning out, Lea abandoned Kang and became closely allied to Sun. He actually accompanied Sun to China when Sun was named president of the Republic of China. Although Mama never mentioned Lea, apparently Papa knew him. It is a tragedy that we never heard from Papa himself about his part in these historical events. We didn't care enough, or know enough, to question him. Mama told us what she remembered, but this was sometimes fragmentary. She did recall what an impact Liang's visit had on him. The two men sat up all night talking; the herb business was neglected during the week or 10 days of Liang's visit. Undoubtedly, they talked about the ascendancy of Sun Yat-sen, Kang's bitter political enemy.

I was born at 6:15 a.m. on the morning of February 16, 1905. Mrs. Mueller, the midwife, didn't have time to get to the house because I was born so fast. Mrs. Brooker helped deliver me and cut the cord. Papa (and probably Mama also) was disappointed to have another girl. E Bok Foo, who had reacted so angrily when Lillie was born, must have been disgusted. One of Papa's patients gave me the name of "Mamie," because it was easy for my parents to pronounce.

When I was three months old, one of the highlights of Papa's life in America occurred. Kang Yu-wei came to Los Angeles to visit and rest. The two had been in touch by correspondence; Kang sent Papa poems describing the scenery of the countries he visited, as well as letters describing the progress of the reform movement. Papa was active in making arrangements for the visit.

Mama described Papa as being *din din day* (sort of crazy) at the prospect of seeing his revered teacher again. It was a memorable visit for the entire Chinese community. There were many who supported Kang's cause of constitutional monarchy in China, and they were eager to pay him homage.

The welcoming party at the train station included not only prominent Chinese, but also representatives of the bench, the Chamber of Commerce, and the military. Kang was accompanied by an interpreter and other members of his entourage. He wore his usual Chinese attire of long gown and vest (he never wore Western attire), and he still had his queue. This was strange, because one of the reforms he had urged was the abolishment of the queue. "Among all the nations of the world we are the strangest," he had said. "We are like a race of animals in that we have tails on our heads."

Our parents were present at a banquet which was described in glowing terms in the *Los Angeles Times:*

> The greatest banquet ever given in Chinatown took place last night in a little banquet hall on Marchessault Street in honor of Kang Yu-wei, who is without doubt the most illustrious living Chinese, the premier of China for a hundred days and a fugitive from the wrath of the Empress with a quarter of a million blood money on his head. . . . As he entered the banquet hall the Chinese fell back in awe-struck lines, leaving a path through to the table, which was set back against the flaming embroidery of the Chinese Imperial banner. . . . His entrance was the most gracious act imaginable.

Toasts were exchanged, and Kang gave a speech. This was the first of many banquets honoring the visiting celebrity, given not only by Chinese, but by leading citizens of Los Angeles.

Papa hosted a large banquet in Kang's honor at "903." This was such a momentous occasion that Mama gave me (an infant of three months) sleeping pills so I would not disturb the guests by crying. I was asleep when Lillie and I were brought into the presence of the great man. In Cantonese dialect Kang is pronounced *Hong* and Papa always addressed Kang as Hong Sing Sung (Teacher Hong). Now he said, "Hong Sing Sung, our youngest daughter has been nameless awaiting your arrival. Would you do her the honor of giving her a Chinese name?" Kang thought a moment, then said, "Let her be called *Law Lan* (Pink Flower)." I slept long after the guests had departed, and Mama worried that she had silenced me forever.

Kang was weary from his travels and wanted to rest. A small house was rented for him across from Westlake Park (now MacArthur Park), at that time a beautiful tranquil haven in the city, but now a mecca for transients and the homeless. He didn't care for American food, so Mama had our cook make his favorite Chinese dishes of steamed chicken and duck. His favorite tea was *yum cum cha* or heart tea, an expensive brew made of the core of trees grown in China. It was believed to enrich the blood and renew energy. Papa visited Kang frequently. They had long discussions about Kang's persisting dream of modernizing China. He still hoped for a *coup d'etat* that would topple Old Buddha and restore Emperor Kuang-hsu to the throne. The problem was how to overthrow Old Buddha. Sometimes Kang and Papa would stay up all night talking, not only about politics but about literature, in which both had a passionate interest. During his exile, Kang had written voluminously, including his most important book, *Ta-tung Shu* (Book of the Great Community), which set forth his almost startlingly modern, utopian ideas on the world he would like to see. Papa spent more time with Kang than he had with Liang, with the subsequent neglect of the herb business.

Mama had a keen interest in the modernization movement. Kang called her his *nir hok sung* (girl scholar) and wrote a poem to her, which unfortunately has been lost. He was sympathetic with her liberal ideas of education for women in China. Despite his own modern theories, he did not go as far as monogamy — he had a wife and two concubines. Apparently, he was not much of a family man. The book *Ta-tung Shu* advocated rearing of children at public expense so that families would no longer be necessary. It is difficult to imagine our parents, who strongly adhered to the Chinese family system, agreeing with these theories. Kang held an open air meeting in Chinatown which was well attended; Mama said he was a good speaker, spicing his talk with humor. He praised the Emperor as a brilliant man and assailed Old Buddha, criticizing the Chinese people for submitting to her domination. He said the Japanese were patriotic and put their country first, whereas the Chinese were "scattered like the sands," thinking only of themselves, not of the country.

Kang was a follower of Confucius, whom he regarded as a reformer. His Confucian theories greatly influenced Papa, and Mama as well. He was so wrapped up in his reform movement and his writings that he neglected himself, Mama said. He cared nothing about appearances or clothes. When his colleagues saw that his attire was getting shabby, they would buy him new clothes. Kang said Los Angeles was his favorite American city. He rested here two or three months before embarking on his tour of the country to get support for the reform movement. Years later, he wrote a poem about his home in Los Angeles. It was framed and hung in the library of our home. Sadly, it was somehow lost, but this is a translation (Kang did not read or write English):

> *I remember my home near Westlake Park,*
> *I think of the old faces I saw there,*
> *Does my home still stand? Do footprints show*
> *   on the floor?*
> *Do brambles grow at the threshold?*
> *My thoughts go back,*
> *I see the spring flowers, the moon brightness,*
> *   the dark green vines.*
> *And every day I look over the lake.*

Mama said that four or five years later Kang's oldest daughter, Kang Tung-wei, came to Los Angeles to visit. She was a brilliant woman, a poetess well-versed in Chinese literature. She stayed at Olive Street for a week.

Papa treasured the photograph taken during Kang's Los Angeles visit; Kang in his Chinese attire is seated, and Papa in a formal American suit and carrying a cane is standing beside him. Kang's departure left a void in Papa's life; he said that after the long talks with Kang, and those with Liang Chi-chao, there was no one interesting to talk with. However, Papa soon joined Kang in Chicago and traveled for about a year with the Kang entourage. This was an exciting adventure for Papa. Not only was he with his beloved teacher, but they were received by high officials in every city. In Washington, D.C., they visited Congress and were welcomed at the White House by President Theodore Roosevelt. They went to factories; we have a picture of them with a group of miners in Butte, Montana. And in every city they were wined and dined by the local Empire Reform Society, which Mama called the Bo Wong. She said all their expenses were paid by the Bo Wong. Papa wrote her many letters during the tour, but she didn't save them. (Mama was not sentimental. The only correspondence between the two that we have are letters she wrote him when he was in China in 1921.) There is no record of how much money was raised for the reform movement on this tour.

While Papa was away, an herbalist named Jur Yu Mu took his place. E Bok Foo was in Boston, where he had an office. About this time, a young woman named Sit Gum Kum came to live with us at Olive Street. She had a key role in a bizarre plot to kill Old Buddha, restore the Emperor to power, and allow Kang to return to China. She had met Liang in Shanghai and had stayed at Liang's home in Japan. Sit Gum Kum had made known to Liang her willingness to take part in the plot. It involved her coming to this country to study because it was known that Old Buddha had a liking for returned students. Sit Gum Kum was then to obtain a position in Old Buddha's court and kill her when the opportunity arose. Only a very few of Kang's closest friends knew of her part in this exciting intrigue, which was being planned in our home. Although Sit Gum Kum had come to this country in the same year Mama did, she studied in San Francisco before moving to

Los Angeles to stay with us. She was a good companion for Mama — they were about the same age — and she took care of Lillie and me as well as attending Los Angeles High School. The Bo Wong gave her some money, and Papa gave her room and board during the three years she lived with us.

Mama described Sit Gum Kum as *di daum* (courageous to the point of boldness). She was not afraid to drive a horse and buggy and took us on many drives to faraway places like Long Beach and Pasadena. Once, Mama said, we toured all of Los Angeles in a horse-drawn bus. Sit Gum Kum did not have bound feet so she could get around much better than Mama. I dimly remember her as a short, dark woman, quite thin, who, unlike Mama, always wore American clothes, long dresses with high collars and mutton-leg sleeves. She was determined to learn English and hired a private tutor as well as attending school. When she first came to live with us, Mama said Sit Gum Kum often declared, "Old Buddha must be killed," and that she was willing to do it. Then gradually she began to change and started to voice fears for her family if she killed Old Buddha. "I don't care if I get killed," she said, "I expect that. But I don't want to endanger my family."

As it turned out, Kang's *coup d'etat* never took place, but not because of Sit Gum Kum's change of mind. Both Old Buddha and the Emperor died in 1908. There were persistent reports that the Emperor had been poisoned. Sit Gum Kum went to Chicago, attended the University of Chicago, graduated, married a fellow Chinese student, and returned to China. Her husband started a chain of banks. Mama believed Sit Gum Kum had never intended to kill Old Buddha, but had merely offered to do it in order to be sent to this country to study, which was her primary goal.

With his friend the Emperor dead, Kang's hopes for a constitutional monarchy were dimmed. He attempted to revive them even after Sun Yat-sen, his bitter political rival, came to power and established the Republic of China. He spent much time in Japan and did not return to China until 1913. Papa also actively continued his support of Kang's cause. He gave money, room, and board to students from China sympathetic to the Bo Wong. One was named Pomona Chan because he attended Pomona College. He was a tall, thin, good-humored man. Another, K.K.

Wong, attended USC. There were others, none of whom ever repaid Papa. When they left, we never heard from them again, according to Mama.

Another die-hard reformer was Tom She Bin, also an herbalist. Some members of the Chinese community looked askance at him because he had concubines. He visited Papa often to discuss the reform movement and conditions in China. In the backyard at Olive Street, there was a big wooden platform surrounded by plants and bushes. Often on pleasant evenings Papa and his reformer friends, including the students and Jo Lop Way, the druggist, who was also a Bo Wong member, would gather there for long talks. Sometimes Mama would join them, and Lillie and I would play on the platform.

A restaurant called King Joy Low was established in Chicago in 1907 by the reformers in the expectation that it would raise money for the movement. However, judging by letters (translated by Charles Liu) written to Papa from relatives in China, the restaurant was a money-loser. It appeared that Papa had persuaded many relatives, both in his family and Mama's, to buy shares in the restaurant. When they failed to receive the dividends they expected, they wrote asking for an explanation; the letters were urgent, sometimes irate. Exactly what part Papa had in running the restaurant is unknown. However, one relative wrote that Papa said he had made a mistake in choosing the manager, who was wasteful with money. Trying to run a restaurant in Chicago while living in Los Angeles would be difficult, at any rate, and Papa was not a good businessman. Even Kang Yu-wei was critical of the way Papa ran the restaurant. It was the only rift that occurred in their friendship. Yet the restaurant stayed in business long after the reformist cause, for which it was founded, had died.

When Kang finally accepted the fact that there was no following for his ideas, he settled in Shanghai, where he lectured and wrote. An admirer of Kang and Liang Chi-chao was Mao Tse-tung, who said that Kang's best-known work, *Ta-tung Shu*, advocated world communism. Kang died in 1927, long before Communist China came into being. Papa died in 1931. It is interesting to conjecture what they would have thought of modern day China. Mama, who died in 1957, opposed Communism, and I believe Papa would have also.

It is an irretrievable loss that we have no first-hand account from Papa of this strange and fascinating chapter of his and Mama's lives. Not until we were gathering notes for this family history were we even aware that a plot that would have changed the history of China was being hatched and discussed in our house at 903 S. Olive Street.

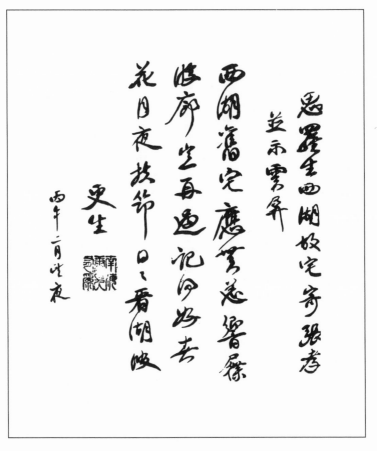

Poem composed and written by Kang Yu-wei, commemorating the occasion of his visit to Tom Leung (translation on page 54). Courtesy UCLA Oriental Library.

GROWING UP

CHAPTER 10

Growing Up

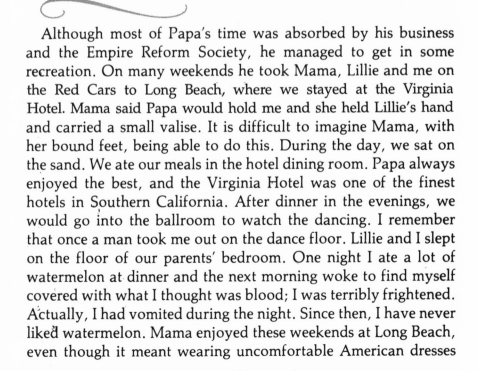

Although most of Papa's time was absorbed by his business and the Empire Reform Society, he managed to get in some recreation. On many weekends he took Mama, Lillie and me on the Red Cars to Long Beach, where we stayed at the Virginia Hotel. Mama said Papa would hold me and she held Lillie's hand and carried a small valise. It is difficult to imagine Mama, with her bound feet, being able to do this. During the day, we sat on the sand. We ate our meals in the hotel dining room. Papa always enjoyed the best, and the Virginia Hotel was one of the finest hotels in Southern California. After dinner in the evenings, we would go into the ballroom to watch the dancing. I remember that once a man took me out on the dance floor. Lillie and I slept on the floor of our parents' bedroom. One night I ate a lot of watermelon at dinner and the next morning woke to find myself covered with what I thought was blood; I was terribly frightened. Actually, I had vomited during the night. Since then, I have never liked watermelon. Mama enjoyed these weekends at Long Beach, even though it meant wearing uncomfortable American dresses and shoes. The hotel managers and workers, as well as guests who frequented the hotel, came to know us and we were always warmly welcomed.

Around this time, our parents would occasionally go to the theater. They especially liked to see Kolb and Dill, comedians who were popular then, at the Majestic Theater at Ninth and Broadway. They would walk there, with Papa holding Mama's arm. Again, it is hard to envision Mama walking that distance. Lillie and I waited up for them, entertaining ourselves by dressing up in Mama's clothes. When it was time for them to come home, we would watch for them from the window of the second floor "red room" until we could see them strolling down the street. It was deserted by that time, lit by one dim streetlight at the intersection in front of our house. By then, Lillie and I would usually be "Mama sick," a term we used when we missed and wanted Mama, and would be so happy to see her and Papa on the way home. I doubt that Mama understood much of the show. She went along mostly because Papa wanted her to; he hated going anywhere alone. Sometimes they went to the Orpheum at Eighth and Broadway, to see the vaudeville. Compared to the stay-at-home life Mama led later on, she was a gadabout during this time when she had only two children.

Mrs. Brooker stayed with us three years. She was followed by Sit Gum Kum, who was not a full time nurse; she looked after Lillie and me only when her studies permitted. Our next nursemaid was Amelia Lee, who didn't stay long. Her place was taken by her sister, Myra. The Lees were an old Los Angeles family, and we kept up a life-long friendship.

Papa was so disappointed that I wasn't a boy that he wanted to dress me in boy's clothes. I was a stubborn child, given to temper tantrums if I didn't get my way. Lillie was the opposite and didn't even fight back when I pulled her hair and hit her. Once I hit Myra Lee when she refused to read the Sunday funny papers over and over. Papa said, "Miss Lee, Mamie's not a girl — she's bad and fights like a tough little boy, so tomorrow you go downtown and buy her boy's clothes." Myra bought me a boy's blue serge coat with brass buttons and a boy's cap with a visor. Far from considering this punishment, I loved this outfit, and was happy to have my picture taken in it with Lillie. My hair was cut short like a boy's, while Lillie wore her hair in braids with ribbons.

My favorite toy was a brown teddy bear, which I carried with me constantly and which I even slept with. One night I had an accident and soiled it. I called Mama in a panic, humiliated and afraid my bear was forever spoiled. Mama cleaned it up so it was as good as ever. She even put perfume on it. I made her promise not to tell anyone, and she never did. I was so ashamed. But after that, I didn't play with the bear much — probably because it reminded me of this humiliating experience. Once, for some reason, I got so angry that I got on the floor, kicked and threw a screaming temper tantrum. Mama, Myra, and others tried to quiet me. Finally, one of the students carried me to my room and shut the door. Mama said I would have to stay there until I was willing to come down and behave. Stubbornly, I refused to come down and stayed in my room most of the day until someone came up and carried me down. Mama said I caused more trouble than the rest of her children.

Later, Lillie and I slept in a tiny bedroom down the hall from our parents. I gave her a bad time because I suffered from insomnia. There was a popular dance hall called Solomon's on Grand Avenue and Ninth Street. I could hear the music from the band, and when it stopped, I knew it was midnight, and the dance hall was closed. It made me terribly lonely, as though I were the only one awake in the whole world. The sight of Lillie sleeping peacefully made it worse. I would pull her hair or pinch her until she sleepily opened her eyes. She never struck back at me but struggled to keep awake; otherwise, I would keep pinching her. When she was wide awake, I would say, "Let's call Mama." So we would both chant in a loud voice, "Mama, *gwa lay*" (Mama, come here) until Mama would come padding down the dark hallway. She would soothe and comfort us. Some nights we called her several times, but she never scolded or was impatient. I could usually fall asleep after she came; Mama represented comfort, security, a haven of peace. Many, many years later, I met the owner of Solomon's dance hall. He was Fred Solomon, who owned a lot of land in Topanga Canyon, where I was living, and still live. I mentioned to him his famous dance hall and the part it had played in my childhood.

Our brother Taft was born about 10 a.m. on March 30, 1909. The secretary for Papa and E Bok Foo at the time was a Mrs. Renee. She told me that the stork had brought me a baby brother. I ran out onto the porch looking for the stork, which was more interesting to me than a baby. After looking in vain, I demanded of Mrs. Renee where the stork was. To others in the household, Taft's birth was cause for great jubilation. E Bok Foo, who had been disgusted at the birth of two girls (he paid us no attention at all), yelled "Boy, a boy!" to Papa, who was out in the yard. Papa was beaming. I'm sure Mama was happy, too. There was a big *mun yirt* (month-old) birthday party for Taft at which he was given many gifts, including *gum hee* (gold jewelry). He was named after President Taft, whom Papa admired greatly. He and Mama pronounced it "Taf-u." Mama believed in dressing her babies warmly. They all wore flannel wrappers around their tummies and long stockings pinned to their diapers, even in summer. To keep their heads warm, she made satin caps, with a hole in the center. For special occasions, she sewed gold ornaments around the caps. For the first month or so, Papa hired a nurse to take care of the newborn. Her name was Mrs. Sylvester, and she wore a starched uniform and cap. She always seemed to be hemming diapers (of course this was long before the day of disposables). Occasionally, she would let me help, which I considered a rare honor.

Taft was a quiet baby, and when he got to the crawling stage, Mama tied bells around his neck so he wouldn't get stepped on, especially when steaming, hot medicine was being brought into the dining room for patients. Lillie and I were not jealous of the new baby, but he annoyed us by crawling around and knocking down the houses we built with blocks. When he was a few months old, Taft broke out with a bad case of eczema. The rash was oozing and red and nothing seemed to help. I was afraid his ear was going to fall off. Papa finally called in an American doctor (the first time he had ever done so), but he couldn't help either. Mama claims she cleared it up by using Cuticura soap.

Our home at Olive Street seemed enormous to me. Lillie and I had several favorite places to play. One was the closet under the steps leading to the second floor. It made an ideal playhouse because it was angled so it was like two rooms. There were windows in the bigger room, which looked onto the front porch. This was our "parlor," and we put curtains up and had tea parties on a little table. We served weak tea and sections of orange. The back room was tiny and dark, and there we set up our "toilet." Sometimes we would invite two neighborhood boys — Vernon, who lived next door, and Glen, who lived down the street — to join us at tea. Invariably, we would fight with one or the other, and he would be banished from our playhouse. We would put paper across the windows so he couldn't peek in.

Another favorite nook was under a chaise lounge–type sofa in one of the downstairs parlors. There was a space where we would play with our paper dolls. Cutting out paper dolls was a passion with us. We would go through magazines and cut out pictures of food, furniture, and clothes. We had bushels of stuff which we kept in Mama's closet. Playing with paper dolls or other toys was the one thing Lillie liked — she didn't care much about playing games. I don't remember our playing together outdoors. Myra Lee had two younger sisters, Dorothy and Laura, who were approximately the same ages as Lillie and I. Once in a while in the evenings, Myra would bring them over. They were shy and so were we, so almost the whole evening would pass before we would start playing, and then it would be time for them to go home. By then, we would be having a great time playing games like "department store" and would hate to stop. We'd say we would start playing at once the next time, but it was always the same story. Laura and I grew to be close friends, especially when we were teenagers.

We had all kinds of toys, many given us by patients. At Christmas, we received so many that Mama would put some of them away. She sent some to China, saying children there had no such toys. I was greedy — I wanted to keep them all. I especially remember a miniature store which we were allowed to play with only on special occasions. I couldn't get enough dolls and played with them till I was 13. My last one was chosen from the Montgomery Ward catalogue — a baby doll with baby clothes and a pacifier. I could hardly wait for it to come, and was elated when it finally arrived. Yet I didn't play with it much — the anticipation was better than the reality.

Lillie and I had no pets. Once a patient brought me a little, black puppy, thinking I would love it. I was afraid of it, and, when it started to chase me around the dining room table, I screamed and cried so loudly that the patient had to take the dog away, much to my relief. I'm sure our parents were relieved because they didn't care for animals, especially in the house.

Mama dressed Lillie and me in long underwear and long, black stockings, even in the summer. We struggled to keep our stockings smooth over the long underwear. Our dresses had long sleeves and high necks. Our clothes were bought by Myra and sometimes by Hallowell. Once Papa went along with Myra to buy us shoes, which we wore out quickly. "Give them iron shoes," he told the salesgirl, who looked bewildered. "He means *sturdy* shoes — shoes that will last," Myra explained. I longed for a dress with a low neck and short sleeves. Finally, I got my wish when I was five or six years old. Papa paid a woman to give Mama sewing lessons at home and bought her a good treadle sewing machine (electricity was not in general use then). One of the first things Mama made was a dress for me with short sleeves and a bloused waist. I called it my "hungry dress," for what reason I don't know, and loved it dearly. We persuaded Mama to let us give up the long underwear, but we wore long stockings (though we were allowed white rather than black) and high shoes all during our childhood. Socks and low shoes were not in fashion then.

Papa thought Mama should learn to cook American food, so he hired a woman to teach her. Mama had never cooked at all; in China it had never been expected that she would have to do such a menial thing. The teacher bought kitchen utensils, a large cooking apron (which almost hid Mama), and the Boston Cook Book, which, of course, she couldn't read. But Mama didn't care for American food and took little interest in learning to prepare it; so the lessons stopped. Later on, Lillie and I made good use of the cook book, which was the cooking Bible of those times. Had we kept it, it would be a collector's item now. Eventually, Mama did learn to cook, just by watching others, and prepared excellent

Chinese dishes, as well as a few American ones. No one could make bread pudding like Mama's; she made up her own recipe. Her baked custards were so tender, never watery or overcooked. It's odd she made these dishes since they contained milk, which she never drank. We never had bottled milk in the house. We children went from condensed milk to tea and coffee. Once Lillie made creamed carrots in her cooking class at Grand Avenue school. That night she was sick and vomited. We had never eaten carrots, and the very idea of carrots cooked with milk was revolting. It made me sick just to think of it. We weren't accustomed to such food, and Lillie vowed she would never eat anything like that again.

Our meals were Chinese, three times a day, beginning with *jook* (rice gruel) in the morning. Papa liked rich food, and our dinners were like banquets with a variety of dishes, including squab, duck, or fish, and an assortment of vegetables. I preferred American food — despite my dislike of carrots — and disdained the succulent dishes. Many times, I would eat plain rice with tea poured over it, much to the dismay of Mama, who considered this unhealthful. The one Chinese food I did like was *foo yer*, salted bean curd. Once when we had no *foo yer*, I got down on the floor and threw one of my temper tantrums, kicking and screaming, disrupting both the women's and men's dining rooms. One of the students had to take me up to my room. When I was old enough to go to the store by myself, I would sometimes wheedle a nickel from Mama and go to the delicatessen at the corner of Ninth and Grand. There, I would buy mashed potatoes and gravy, served on a wooden scoop with a little wooden spoon. To me, that first taste of potatoes bathed in gravy was so much more luscious than the flavorsome Chinese dishes I spurned.

Lessons – Chinese and Music

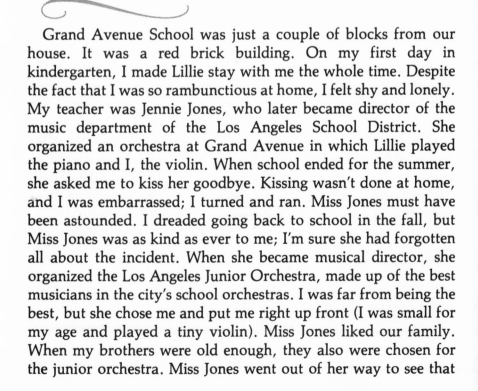

Grand Avenue School was just a couple of blocks from our house. It was a red brick building. On my first day in kindergarten, I made Lillie stay with me the whole time. Despite the fact that I was so rambunctious at home, I felt shy and lonely. My teacher was Jennie Jones, who later became director of the music department of the Los Angeles School District. She organized an orchestra at Grand Avenue in which Lillie played the piano and I, the violin. When school ended for the summer, she asked me to kiss her goodbye. Kissing wasn't done at home, and I was embarrassed; I turned and ran. Miss Jones must have been astounded. I dreaded going back to school in the fall, but Miss Jones was as kind as ever to me; I'm sure she had forgotten all about the incident. When she became musical director, she organized the Los Angeles Junior Orchestra, made up of the best musicians in the city's school orchestras. I was far from being the best, but she chose me and put me right up front (I was small for my age and played a tiny violin). Miss Jones liked our family. When my brothers were old enough, they also were chosen for the junior orchestra. Miss Jones went out of her way to see that we got to rehearsals and to performances. I think she liked having Chinese students in her orchestra.

My best friend at Grand Avenue School was Bessie Bergman, a Jewish girl with dark, curly hair and gold earrings in her pierced ears. Sometimes she would come to my house, and we would play hopscotch on the cement walk leading to the front porch. I was disconsolate at leaving her when we moved from Olive Street.

To please Mrs. Findlay, Lillie and I went to Sunday school for a while. The church (I don't remember which domination) was only a few blocks from the house. We were given money to put in the collection box. Instead, we stopped at a candy store and bought candy; we had nothing to contribute when we got to Sunday school. We were bored with the talk about religion, which was completely foreign to us, and soon persuaded our parents to let us skip Sunday school. They didn't care one way or another; if we'd enjoyed it, we could have continued. In regard to religion, Mama once said: "If you do what's right, that's good enough. You don't have to go to church for that." When we were teenagers we did go to church in Chinatown on Easter and special occasions, but it was solely for social purposes. We referred to religious people as "God guys."

Lillie started piano lessons with Elsie Parsons when she was five. Miss Parsons may or may not have been a good teacher, but she was a beautiful person, both in looks and in spirit. She lived with her mother, a young brother, and several sisters, all of whom were exceptionally good-looking. We came to know the family well, and I admired them profoundly. Our friends Dorothy and Laura Lee were also pupils of Miss Parsons. About twice a year, she gave recitals in which all her students participated. The recitals were held at our house in the *hoong fong*, and they were the highlights of the year for Lillie and me, even though I wasn't one of the students. We helped Miss Parsons set up rows of chairs for the guests. After the performance, we played games and had refreshments prepared by Miss Parsons. I looked forward to those refreshments — they were always delicious, beautifully served, and different from anything I'd ever tasted. Each Christmas, Miss Parsons gave our family a hand-painted piece of china, her own handiwork. We considered them too beautiful to use and displayed them in the china cabinet. As the years went by, we gathered quite a collection of her plates, dishes, and cups and saucers. I wish I knew what happened to them.

I was about five when I started to take violin lessons. Daisy Walters was my teacher. She was the antithesis of Miss Parsons — a tall, homely woman, drab, with no personality. I hardly said a word to her during the lessons on Tuesdays and Fridays. The violin was a difficult instrument for me, even though I had the smallest violin obtainable. Miss Walters had me play the Largo, and I came to hate it. At first, I practiced diligently, but when it seemed to make no difference in my playing, I gave up practicing. Miss Walters charged $1.25 a lesson. With such an unenthusiastic pupil, she must have found the lessons as dull as I, but they went on for years, a waste of Papa's money. I did enjoy playing in the school orchestra, which I continued to do through high school. When we were in high school and college, Lillie and I played for groups such as the Chinese Students' Club, but my performance was amateurish; I was always afraid a string would break while I was playing, or when I tuned the instrument. The violin had never been my choice — it was Papa's. He wanted each of his children to play a different instrument. I liked the piano and finally persuaded my parents to let me take piano lessons with Miss Parsons, but I was not allowed to stop playing the violin. When I eventually did stop, I put my violin up on a shelf in my closet and never did play it again.

Lillie and I were five or six years old when we started taking Chinese lessons. By this time, English was already our first language. Our parents always spoke Chinese at home, but we were surrounded by English-speaking nurses, secretaries, and schoolmates. Unfortunately, we did not grow up bilingual, as some Chinese-Americans did. Our first (of many) teachers was Liang Hing Lern, one of the students who lived in the little house in the backyard. Our parents were very anxious that we learn to speak, read, and write Chinese; they were dismayed that we were becoming so Americanized. Papa practiced his calligraphy constantly, and he won the reputation of being the finest calligrapher on the West Coast. He would take my hand, show me exactly how to hold the brush, guide it in writing the characters, and explain the precedence of the strokes. That is the one thing in my years of Chinese lessons that has stuck with me. Otherwise, the lessons were an ordeal that I grew to hate. I didn't see why I had to learn Chinese when I was always going to live in America. The only way I could remember the characters was to write the American phonetic sound beside them. Our teachers should never have allowed me to do this, but they were all lenient. None of them tried to make the lessons interesting. For a long time, we took lessons only during the summer because we were so busy with school and our music lessons. By the time the next summer came, I would have forgotten all I had learned the summer before. Lillie was better than I, perhaps because she did not rebel against learning Chinese like I did. I wanted to be like my schoolmates. I didn't like being different. Being Chinese meant being different, so I developed a mental block against learning Chinese and eating Chinese food. Sometimes on the way to school, small boys would jeer at Lillie and me, calling "Chink" or "skibee" (meaning Japanese). We would cross the street to avoid them. I don't recall that there were any other Asians in our school, so we were a novelty. I would dread coming to the chapter in our geography lesson dealing with China. Some of the children would then turn their heads and look at me. I didn't tell anyone, not even Lillie, and certainly not my parents, about my feelings. Our parents wanted us to be proud of our heritage; they would have been shocked at how I felt. Despite this, I had an intense loyalty to the family. It wasn't until college that I outgrew these ambivalent feelings. Then I began to envy my friends who could speak Chinese fluently as well as English. I took a course in Mandarin and got an "A" only because the professor was so easy. But I promptly forgot all I learned and to this day cannot understand a word in Mandarin.

Our parents spoke the *sahm yup* dialect of Cantonese, and that is what we were taught. Communication with them was difficult. We children developed a sort of "pidgin" Chinese and English in speaking to our parents. We knew the common, everyday words in Chinese, such as "eat," "sleep," "go out," "like," "dislike," etc.

In talking to Mama, we would speak in sentences that were a mixture of English and Chinese. Though she spoke little English, she understood what we said to her. Our level of communication was low. We could talk about what to have for dinner or what to buy at the store, but we couldn't discuss ideas. Our parents never asked us what we were studying in school; we wouldn't have had the vocabulary to explain. However, they wanted to make sure we were doing well and always looked at our report cards. They could read the alphabet and knew that "A" meant excellent, and "F" meant failure. I was eager to curry the good opinion of my parents and my teachers and tried my best for "A"s, and usually succeeded. I had a photographic memory which stood me well in examinations, but in a few days I would have forgotten what I had learned. So my reputation for being a good student was really not earned; I probably didn't learn as much as students who got poorer grades but retained what they studied. We would take our report cards to Mama, who would show them to Papa or tell him how we had progressed. We had practically no communication with Papa. In many ways, he was the typical, aloof, Chinese father, whom we regarded with awe and respect; but he was also most indulgent, and whatever we wanted, we usually received. We went to Mama for everything; she was our "middleman" and would relay our wishes to Papa. She was always there for us, gentle and understanding. Papa paid little attention to babies. We couldn't imagine him diapering a baby, or giving it its bottle as American fathers did. Sometimes he would chuck a baby under the chin and say *Ung Ung goo* (Chinese baby talk). When I was very young, I remember him cracking my knuckles, which he thought was fun but which I didn't like. We would never think of jumping on his lap or calling him "Daddy"; yet we knew he cared about us, and we felt secure in our home. Mama often talked to us about her life in China, but Papa never did. We knew nothing about his boyhood, his family, or his home. During his lifetime, Papa was the dominant person in our household — everyone deferred to him. Mama stayed in the background — as she thought a Chinese wife should do. It was not until some of her letters to him were translated in recent years that her great influence on him was revealed.

CHAPTER 12

More Leungs Are Born

William (we always called him "Wum") was born on September 27, 1910. Since he was the second boy, there wasn't a fuss made over his birth. William was a very active baby. At a very young age, he could crawl out of his crib and find where Mama had hidden the candy. Mama said he was like a monkey. Less than a year later, on September 18, 1911, Howard was born. Since William was using the crib, Howard had to sleep in a buggy, a fact that caused his short stature, Mama said. Lillie and I thought it was wonderful to wake up in the morning and find a new baby in the house. Mrs. Sylvester would be there too, in her starchy uniform, to take care of the baby. Mama would be in bed, with a bowl of chicken and wine at her side, and the "new baby smell" would permeate the room. I hated to go to school, and I would rush home as soon as it was over so I could lie on the bed and watch the infant.

The boys were named after President William Howard Taft, whom Papa greatly respected. A letter was sent to the president telling him of his three namesakes, and a gracious response was received from President Taft. The boys also had Chinese names, of course, all beginning with the character "Way." None of us were ever called by our Chinese names, even by our parents.

Mama had given up going out so much after Taft was born. We no longer took our weekend trips to Long Beach. After Mrs. Sylvester stayed her customary several weeks, Mama took care of the babies. She didn't trust the nurses to look after them. I loved to watch her bathe them in the big bathroom sink, powder them, and dress them, beginning with the flannel binder around their tummies. When they were all dressed and wrapped in a blanket, she would let me hold them while she prepared the bottle of condensed milk. They smelled so sweet and clean. There was no such thing as Gerber's baby food, and the babies had nothing but milk. When they were six months old, they started getting hot cereal like Cream of Wheat. Mama never had to wash the diapers and clothes.

Myra Lee didn't stay with us long; she got more lucrative work as a seamstress. After Papa tried in vain to find another Chinese nurse, a white nurse was hired to look after Taft, but she was unsatisfactory for some reason. Then Papa started hiring colored (the term "black" was not used then) maids from the employment agency. We called them *hak gway* (black ghosts). They did the washing on old-fashioned washboards (washing machines were a luxury that came much later), wringing the clothes by hand. Items like sheets and towels and Papa's shirts were sent to a laundry once a week. Our first *hak gway* was named Addie. Then came Mary, who stayed with us for many years, and with whom we kept in touch long after she left. She had Thanksgiving dinner with us in the early 70's, which was the last time we saw her.

Holly was born on December 26, 1912. A patient suggested the name Holly because she was a Christmas baby. After we moved from Olive Street, two more boys were born — Monroe, on April 19, 1915, and Lincoln, on May 30, 1917. In naming these boys, Papa continued his tradition of naming his sons after American presidents. Why he chose to "honor" President Monroe is unknown because he had never voiced any opinion about him; perhaps he liked the sound of the name, which he and Mama both pronounced "Monloe." Lincoln was originally named Bismarck, after the German chancellor, who was one of Papa's heroes. But when World War I broke out, Papa was told it was unwise to have a baby named after a German. The younger children had not been able to pronounce the name Bismarck, and had garbled the name into "Minewa." Everyone began calling him that, too, but it was soon simplified to "Mincie." Papa heeded the advice about Germans and changed Bismarck to Lincoln, who he knew was a great president. No one in the family ever called him Lincoln, and to us he is Mincie to this day.

Occasionally, Lillie and I were awakened in the middle of the night by the sound of activity and whispered talking from the *hoong fong.* We would get up and go running into the "red room." There would be Papa and Mama and some strange men who looked dirty and disheveled. Mama would order us to go back to our room immediately. The next day there would be a new relative or new student in the household. Much later, we learned that these men had been smuggled into the country; they could not enter legally because of the immigration laws. Perhaps Papa's brother, Chuck Ga Sook, and his nephew, whom we called Yum Go, were smuggled in this way. We were too young at the time to remember, but we could sense something secret was going on by the excitement in the voices of our elders and the way Mama put her finger to her lips and "shushed" us to be quiet. I never did learn how the smuggling was arranged, but apparently, Papa paid a couple of men to help get his relatives across the border and over to Olive Street.

E Bok Foo spent much of his time in Oakland, where he had an office with one of his sons, Sahm Go. E Bok Foo had four sons in this country — E Gow, Sahm Gow, Say Gow, and Ng Gow. My favorite was E Gow, or Tom How Wing, who lived for a time in the back house. Say Gow was handsome like his mother. Ng Gow was active in the Empire Reform Society and established his own herb company. Since E Bok Foo was gone so much of the time, Papa was practically the head of the Foo and Wing Herb Company.

Winnie Johnson was Papa's secretary for a short time, followed by her sister, Mabel, who remained with us for many years. The

Johnson sisters — there was a third, Esther — became close friends of our family. Winnie cut off the queue of Gee Sook, the cook, at his request. He had debated the matter for some time. Winnie took him out into the backyard and hacked off the queue. She had told him he must wash his hair, which he had never done, before she would trim it. He complied, and she gave him a haircut.

The Johnsons called Papa's brother, Chuck Ga Sook, "Chicken Soup," a nickname that stuck with him. Chuck was my least favorite relative. He was the opposite of Papa — common-looking, and vulgar in speech. I never saw the two talking together like brothers; they seemed to have nothing in common. Papa opened an office in San Diego and put Chuck in charge, but he was not successful. He could not attract patients; he didn't have the personality to inspire confidence. Although he lived with us, he did not have the same friends as our parents; they never went anywhere together.

By the time Lillie was eight or nine, she assumed responsibilities unusual for one of her age. She began doing the family shopping. Mama would tell her what the younger children needed in the way of clothes, and Lillie would go to Hamburgers and buy them. She developed a good sense of values and knew what was well-made and what was cheap and shoddy. I would tag along with her, but Lillie did all the talking with the salespeople and made the decisions. At times, Papa would have her write business letters when the secretary was not available. Both parents depended on her more and more as she grew older. She was neat and efficient in everything that she did and always dependable. Soon I was playing more with Taft than with her; she was usually busy helping Mama or Papa. I can't imagine what they would have done without her. She was indispensable. In a way, it seemed unfair that she didn't have more of a childhood.

CHAPTER 13

Papa Gets Arrested

Papa did well as an herbalist, too well, in the opinion of the American Medical Association and the Board of Medical Examiners. He and the other Chinese herbalists in Los Angeles at that time were accused of practicing medicine without a license because they used the title "Doctor" and felt the pulse as one way of diagnosis. Papa was a special target and was arrested over 100 times on the misdemeanor charge. "The more he was arrested, the more business he got," Mama said. Sometimes, the police would come one day and arrest him and then return the next, hoping to catch him unaware. The police, at times, used stool pigeons — people pretending to be patients — and would arrest Papa after the usual consultation. Sometimes a whole squad of police would arrive in a patrol car and raid our home. I came to view the AMA and the Board, as well as the police, as our mortal enemies. Papa was unflappable, even the time when he was hauled off in the patrol wagon. He had set up a routine for these crises. As soon as the police came, the secretary phoned A.C. Way of the First National Bank to arrange for bail. (Way was a good friend of

Papa's, was much interested in the Empire Reform Society, and was a leading citizen of Los Angeles.) If the arrest was made on or near a holiday, and it was impossible to get bail from the bank (the police would do this purposely), Papa would get it from Chinatown. He never had to spend any time in jail. Papa's attorneys were Thomas White and Paul Schenck, both well-known. Schenck was called "Crazy Dog," Mama said, because he bared his teeth while arguing in court. Sometimes, Papa would plead guilty and other times go to trial; he lost more times than he won. When patients were called as witnesses, they testified in Papa's favor, according to Mama. He paid a total of approximately $5,000 in fines, she said.

I felt both angered and ashamed at these arrests. Sometimes, there would be a paragraph in the newspaper about the arrest, and I would dread going to school the next day for fear some of my schoolmates or my teachers would have seen it. But the conduct of the police infuriated me. They went through the rooms, handling the art objects, looking at everything, and making remarks. We have a clipping from an unknown newspaper, dated December 11, 1913, and headed "Chinese Herbalist Says He Was Robbed." It reads:

> Two valuable Chinese water pipes of rare design were stolen from the establishment of the Foo and Wing company at 903 S. Olive Street when a squad of officers under the direction of Inspector E. A. Somner of the state medical board raided the place yesterday and arrested T. Leung, a Chinese herbalist, on a charge of practicing medicine without a license.
>
> The matter was brought to the attention of the police today when Dr. Leung sought Detective Burgess and asked the latter to make an effort to locate the missing articles.
>
> The Chinese protested to Detective Burgess of the alleged lax manner in which the raid was conducted, and declared that persons who had no authority were allowed to roam from room to room of his house and handle articles that belonged to his family and had

no connection with the matter involved.

The water pipes were never returned, but a book in which Papa had written all our birth dates was given back to us. There were attempts to pass legislation to legalize herbalists together with chiropractors, who were also having trouble with the AMA, but all attempts failed. The ignominious arrests went on until 1923, long after we had moved to 1619 W. Pico Street. They stopped when Papa discontinued calling himself "Doctor" and was presumably just in the business of selling herbs. He then called the firm the T. Leung Herb Co.

Papa was more successful than other Chinese herbalists because he had a flair for public relations. He took out ads in all the larger Los Angeles newspapers. Every Christmas he sent elaborate cards to all patients, past and present. Seated around the dining room table, several of us were put to work addressing hundreds of cards. He distributed calendars and rulers (I still have one) with T. Leung Herb Co. on them. One of his most successful promotions was T. W. Oil, meaning "Thousand Wonders Oil," described as follows:

> This oil can be used either externally or internally. It is valuable for countless ailments and affections and in every case relief is obtained. Its use is extensive in China, and it is considered one of the most useful household remedies. It is harmless and non-poisonous, and being a fine antiseptic, it protects the body from many dangerous germs, hence it is one of the most valuable and inexpensive remedies in the WORLD.

We called this oil *yer yo* and found it indispensable. I used it for toothaches and headaches, for cuts and insect bites. When I was in China, I tried to get some, without success. I was able to get Tiger Balm, which is similar, but not the pungent, soothing *yer yo* Papa sold for 25¢ to $2.50 per bottle.

All of us were brought up on herbs. When we had colds, we were given a dose of *mo jer*, which seemed to have magical, curative powers. Some members of the family still get *mo jer* from Chinatown. We all dreaded taking the bitter medicine, but fortunately, we were rarely ill. Mama would sit beside us, coaxing and urging us to hurry and drink the cup of brew. I discovered that the best way was to hold my nose and gulp it down all at once; taking small sips only prolonged the ordeal. If one type of medicine didn't help us, Papa would write a different prescription. For sprains and bruises, we were rubbed with *tit da jo*, a pungent liquid that relieved the pain. Mama suffered from *fung sup*, literally "wind wet," or what we called rheumatism. For this, she used a black plaster, softened over steam and applied to the ache. She believed these plasters were the only things that could help her. Papa knew about acupuncture, but he didn't know how to practice it. He would be gratified to know how acupuncture has been accepted in this country, and that Western medicine even looks favorably on many kinds of Chinese herbs. He had always thought that Western medicine and Chinese herbal science were compatible. He had even wished that one of his children would go to medical school, earn an M.D., and go into practice with him. A visit to a hospital in China would have been fascinating for him. There he would have seen a blend of Western and Chinese medicine, with surgery performed using acupuncture as the anesthetic.

None of us eight children had so much as a broken bone. About the worst thing that happened was when Taft had the tip of one of his fingers almost severed by a lawn mower. Mama tried to treat it and bandage it, but Taft was in such pain that an American doctor was called in. By that time, the bandage was stuck to the injured finger, and the doctor had a difficult time removing it. Poor Taft screamed in agony. I stuck my fingers in my ears so I wouldn't hear him. He had to have several visits from the doctor before the finger was healed. Herbs didn't help in a case like this. During Papa's last illness, he first dosed himself with herbs, but when he got steadily worse, he called in a Western doctor to no avail. When Mama suffered a stroke toward the end of her life, her doctor was a Chinese graduate of Loma Linda University.

CHAPTER 14

Holiday Celebrations

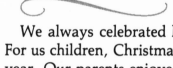

We always celebrated holidays, both American and Chinese. For us children, Christmas was, of course, the biggest day of the year. Our parents enjoyed it enormously too, though there was no religious significance in our celebration. When Lillie and I were very young, we believed in Santa Claus. Who told us this myth, I don't recall, but it was probably a nurse or a secretary. Our parents went along with it, letting us indulge in this American fantasy. One Christmas Eve, we were allowed to spend the night at the home of the Johnson sisters. We were so excited we couldn't sleep. We crept downstairs and saw the Johnsons placing gaily wrapped presents around the tree. That was how Lillie and I found out there was no Santa Claus. This disillusionment was not at all shattering; it didn't dampen our enjoyment of Christmas in the least. So, when the younger children came along, we passed on the Santa story to them. One thing we insisted on was a tree that was tall enough to touch the ceiling. Papa liked a big tree, too. We had a wonderful time decorating it. On Christmas Eve, Lillie and I would get out the packages; we arranged them so that they would surround the tree and almost fill the room. On these occasions, Papa would drop his reserve and be jolly. Sometimes, he and Mama would go downstairs on Christmas Eve and unwrap presents and then re-wrap them. They were worse than the kids — they couldn't wait!

We were overwhelmed with gifts. Mama gave Lillie the money to buy gifts for everyone; Lillie and I spent days Christmas shopping, exploring the toy departments in all the stores; Papa loved the toy departments, too. He never bought dolls or toys for the girls, but for the boys he got expensive train sets, Erector sets and chemistry kits. After the boys opened their gifts, he would monopolize and take over until he got tired of them; then the kids, who had been standing by impatiently, would have their chance. Those childhood Christmases were such festive occasions. Each year I would make a wish to myself that our family would all be together again the next year. Our Christmases are still wonderful. Our numbers have multiplied many times, although many of the older ones are no longer with us.

Thanksgiving was another important holiday. I especially looked forward to it because it was the one time of the year when we had an American feast. We children learned about Thanksgiving at school and would bring home drawings of turkeys and Pilgrims. How much Papa and Mama knew about the origin of the holiday, I don't know, but Papa loved to celebrate and to sit at the head of the table surrounded by family and guests. The cooking was done by the secretary or the nurse because Gee Sook had no knowledge of how to make American dishes. Even though our parents didn't care for turkey because they thought it was too dry, they followed tradition (although once we had a roast pig). Papa liked chestnut dressing, the only part of the dinner he really relished.

The best Thanksgivings were in the years after we moved to 1619 W. Pico Street. Mabel Johnson did the cooking; she loved to eat and was a good cook. I stayed in the kitchen, watching, and was allowed to do such things as sew up the turkey after it was stuffed and peel the yams. Lillie and I set the long dining-room table, which had enough leaves to accommodate 20 people. The table cloth was of the best linen. Papa always liked the finest, including a beautiful set of de Haviland china and heavy sterling silver (I still have two of the serving spoons). Our parents always had a glass of wine with their dinner, but on Thanksgiving, they had three different kinds of wine, including champagne. We placed three crystal wine glasses at each setting; even the children were allowed a taste of champagne. Papa didn't carry out the traditional role of the American father carving the turkey. He considered that a menial task. The bird was sliced in the kitchen and served on a big silver platter. On one memorable Thanksgiving, Papa had menus printed and hired a waiter. We children considered this most impressive.

Papa ignored Easter. We had Easter egg hunts for the younger children, and if we ever went to church, it was for social purposes and not for observing the religious significance of Easter. Until fireworks were illegal, Papa continued his July 4 fireworks display, which he began when he first came to this country.

Winnie Johnson told me that Papa and Mama had a heated argument one Halloween when I was two or three years old. Papa bought a mask and put it on me, wanting to take me out on the street with the other Halloween revelers. I started to cry, and Mama protested that the mask was smothering me. She thought the whole idea about Halloween was utter foolishness. Papa got angry, and they quarreled loudly, with me screaming. Finally, Papa took off the mask, threw it on the floor, and stomped out of the room. Papa liked to follow American customs; he always wanted to celebrate on New Year's Eve. We nearly always had a party, and later on, dances. On the rare occasions when we had no guests, Papa would complain. At midnight, he would take his cornet out on the street and blow a loud blast on it. He loved festivity — *go hing* as he called it.

Chinese New Year was, of course, a big event in our family. Papa would start preparations several months in advance by planting Chinese lily bulbs in blue planters. There were at least a dozen or more, so they could be placed in various rooms of the house. They always seemed to bloom just in time for New Year, and their heady, sweet fragrance filled the house. These were the only flowers he personally planted, and he was very proud of them. Mama would get out the special New Year tablecloth, a red silk embroidered cloth with little glass insets which I thought was the most beautiful thing in the world. On it she would place the gold lacquered dish with many compartments, into which she put different sweets, such as candied ginger, coconut strips, lichee nuts, and sweet and sour plums. The traditional New Year dish was *tsai,* an assortment of vegetables such as hair seaweed, bean threads, snow peas, bamboo shoots, mushrooms, cloud ears fungus, and many others. It required a great deal of chopping, cutting, and cooking, but the result was deliciously flavorful. Sometimes we went to Chinatown to see the fireworks and the lion dance.

At Olive Street in the early days, there was always a constant stream of visitors. Lillie and I would dutifully say *Gong hay fat choy* and the guests would put *lai see* (money wrapped in red paper) in a large straw tray. By the end of the day, the tray would be heaped with wrapped money, not only with coins but with dollar bills. Lillie and I would divide up the money, then Mama would take charge of it, saying it would be put in the bank for us. Actually, I don't think we ever saw this money again, but it didn't matter. We had no idea what money was worth, and if we ever wanted to buy something, we asked and usually got it. None of us were ever given allowances.

Among the beliefs that Mama brought from China were the superstitions that one must have a clean house and one must not have one's hair cut on Chinese New Year. Myra Lee recalled one Chinese New Year when, knowing the household needed a broom, she said to Mama, "Mrs. Leung, I'm going shopping to-day and get that broom you need." Mama looked horrified and shushed her, saying, "No, no, it's New Year!" The next day Papa was arrested for practicing medicine without a license. Mama said, "Miss Lee, this is the bad luck you brought on our house by talking about a broom on New Year." Poor Myra was on the verge of tears. She consulted one of the students in the back house and he explained that this was just an old Chinese superstition.

We also celebrated the Dragon Boat Festival on the fifth day of the fifth month, and the Autumn Festival during the full moon of the equinox at the end of September. We were never told the origin of these holidays, but they were times of feasting. There were no boats connected with our Dragon Boat Festival, but we had *joong*, a kind of Chinese tamale, made with *naw mai* (sweet rice), *lop cherng* (Chinese sausage), chestnuts, salted duck eggs, *hah mai* (dried shrimp), mushrooms, and other choice ingredients. They were wrapped in ti leaves and boiled. There was an art to this wrapping. Mama finally learned how to do it, but making *joong* was an enormous lot of work that has not been mastered by many Chinese-American cooks. At the Autumn Festival, we ate round moon cakes, some sweet, and some filled with black *do sa*.

Birthdays were always observed with presents and a big dinner. If the birthday was not celebrated on the day itself, we were always careful that the observance was held *before*, not afterwards. It was bad luck to celebrate afterwards — another Chinese superstition that some members of our family still follow.

Although Papa always had a glass of wine with dinner, he did not drink to excess. I can remember only two times when he got drunk. Once was when Sit Gum Kum was living with us, and Papa entertained with a big dinner for guests from Chicago, members of the Empire Reform Society. After eating, the men played the "finger game," in which the loser had to down a glass of wine. There was a lot of shouting connected with this game, as the men tried to guess how many fingers his partner would thrust up. There were also many toasts to China, such as "May she live to be 10,000 years old." After an evening of this, Papa passed out, one guest burned his own face with a cigarette, and everyone got uproariously drunk. Even Mama drank too much and got sick. Apparently, Sit Gum Kum was the only one who stayed half sober. She took care of Lillie and me, who were sitting, frightened by all the noise, on the steps by the dining room. Mama laughed as she recalled it. Apparently, it must have been one wild party.

The only other time I recall Papa drinking too much was when he went to a dinner in Chinatown and came home drunk. Mama usually drank very little, but both our parents enjoyed fine wines. Papa's face got red when he drank too much — a trait he passed on to the younger Leungs.

"1619"

CHAPTER 15

Planning and Building

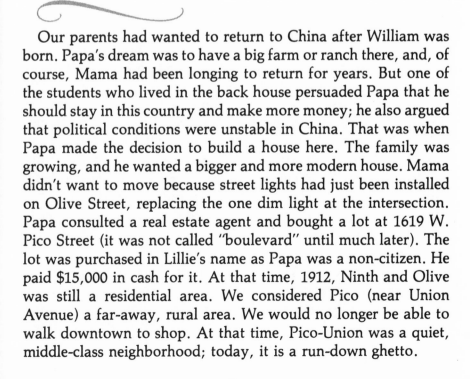

Our parents had wanted to return to China after William was born. Papa's dream was to have a big farm or ranch there, and, of course, Mama had been longing to return for years. But one of the students who lived in the back house persuaded Papa that he should stay in this country and make more money; he also argued that political conditions were unstable in China. That was when Papa made the decision to build a house here. The family was growing, and he wanted a bigger and more modern house. Mama didn't want to move because street lights had just been installed on Olive Street, replacing the one dim light at the intersection. Papa consulted a real estate agent and bought a lot at 1619 W. Pico Street (it was not called "boulevard" until much later). The lot was purchased in Lillie's name as Papa was a non-citizen. He paid $15,000 in cash for it. At that time, 1912, Ninth and Olive was still a residential area. We considered Pico (near Union Avenue) a far-away, rural area. We would no longer be able to walk downtown to shop. At that time, Pico-Union was a quiet, middle-class neighborhood; today, it is a run-down ghetto.

The architect Papa chose was H. A. Kerton, one of his patients. Papa told Kerton he wanted a large, two-story house with an office, many bedrooms, and a basement, and he didn't want to spend more than $3,000. Kerton said that was impossible. Papa told him to go ahead and prepare the sketches. Kerton did so and gave an estimate of $9,200, to which Papa made no objections. Many changes were made in the plans, the biggest being the addition of a third story and roof garden. The total cost, including the lot, the house, and all new furnishings, came to $30,000, which Papa paid in cash.

Kerton asked Papa why he had accepted the $9,200 estimate without demurring when he had insisted he wanted to pay no more than $3,000. "If I had said $9,200, you would have designed a $20,000 house," Papa answered. Kerton hired a Mr. Wilson to be the building contractor.

Some of the neighbors on Pico Street were unhappy about having a Chinese family in their midst. There was a rumor that Papa was going to build a hospital. A petition was circulated in the neighborhood. Kerton told the protestors that there was no hospital planned, only a home that would improve the area. Just who instigated the protest, we never knew, but I suspected it was the aristocrats of the neighborhood, the Jones family. They lived just across the street from us in a big, stately house, set far back and surrounded by rolling lawns and gardens. The family consisted of the elder Joneses, their son, a lieutenant in the Los Angeles Police Department, his wife, and their little girl named Edna. Edna was right out of a story book, with long blonde curls, and always beautifully dressed. They had a big car, and any time the ladies went out, they were hatted, furred, and high-heeled. I was always curious about the Joneses, but, of course, they had nothing to do with us. Nothing came of the petition. We came to know the neighbors on our right and left, and had a nodding acquaintance with others.

Papa was obsessed with plans for the "new house." Kerton often came by at night to confer with him. They sat at a table in the "red room" poring over the drawings. Mama, Lillie, and I would join them. It was very exciting. Kerton showed us where our room was in the drawings. We insisted that we each have our

View of the second home and office, 1619 West Pico.

own closet. Mama took no part in the discussions; she left it to Papa, and he knew just what he wanted.

In addition to the frequent night meetings, Papa wrote letters (through Mabel Johnson) to Kerton and Wilson whenever he had a new idea about the house. For example, the library was to be on the third floor, so he wanted that floor built higher and larger to make the library large enough to accommodate all his books. He also wanted the basement made larger "so the children could use it as a playroom in the summertime." Kerton, replying in long hand, rejected the larger third floor, pointing out that the house would be too high in proportion to its width. He sent sketches showing that the library was of "exceptional size" (22' x 14') with "ample wall space for bookcases." The basement was enlarged at a total cost of $660. Papa would also make long lists of the things he wanted, such as sliding doors for the herb room and the sleeping porch, a laundry chute from the second floor to the basement where the laundry tubs were located, and a sandpile in the basement. There was much correspondence about the custom-built wood range for the kitchen. Gee Sook, the cook, refused to use anything but a wood stove. Kerton made a sketch from the stove at Olive Street and from Papa's suggestions. It had a large cooking surface, and at one end, a round hole which held a big wok for cooking rice. Papa found a company in Los Angeles to build the range. A woodshed was constructed in the backyard near the utility porch. Even on the hottest days, Gee Sook would fire up the range, ignoring the brand new gas stove next to it.

There was also much controversy over the heating system. It started out as a gas-fired steam boiler, but this proved unsatisfactory, and an oil-burning, steam-heating system was installed, costing $1,196. This was a complicated project, requiring the excavation of the front yard to allow installation of pipes to the furnace room in the basement. The tank fueling the burner had a capacity of 1,200 gallons. Whenever it had to be refilled, the pipe opening in the front lawn was uncovered. A huge oil truck would come lumbering up and the oil would gush in. We children found this operation fascinating to watch.

Papa must have been a difficult client to work with; he had so many suggestions and changes. It was amazing how much information on house building he amassed, down to the smallest detail. Because of his language problems, he took Lillie with him so she could explain to Kerton what he wanted. Lillie went with him to view houses so he could get ideas. He had, for example, wanted alternate dark and light strips for the hardwood floors throughout the house, but decided on a solid color after viewing homes. Often, he would send Kerton to competing companies, such as water heater dealers, to discover their relative merits. He always insisted on knowing the price of everything, but he chose what he thought was best, not the cheapest.

"If Dr. Leung made a statement, he lived up to it," Kerton said. He recalled once going to look at light fixtures with Papa. Afterwards they went to a Chinese restaurant for lunch. "Dr. Leung insisted that I order chop suey. For himself he ordered a mammoth porterhouse steak which he ate without vegetables or any side dishes." Once, soon after "1619" was completed, Kerton stopped by and had dinner. Afterwards, Papa invited him to go to the library where he prepared some $50-a-pound tea over an alcohol lamp. He showed Kerton two thick volumes in Chinese which dealt with the subject of how to boil water to make tea. Kerton said the tea was absolutely colorless and had an almost indiscernible flavor, but left his mouth with a smooth sensation, as though it had been cleansed. On Christmas, Papa gave Kerton a silver belt buckle and Mrs. Kerton a fine silk shawl. Papa told Kerton he would retain his services when he built a house in China.

When building began, there was an architect's drawing of the house in a newspaper with the following article:

> Construction has begun on a large residence planned by H.A. Kerton for Dr. T. Leung and having as its site a 50-foot lot at No. 1619 West Pico Street. The house will be three stories high in the front, with two stories and a roof garden at the rear. It will contain 15 rooms. On the first floor provision is made for an office, reception hall, parlor, dining room, breakfast room and kitchen. The second floor will contain a parlor, five bedrooms, and a sleeping porch. On the third floor will be a library and two bedrooms. The baths will be finished in tile. The downstairs will be in red birch, while the upper stories will be in white enamel.

Papa took Lillie and me frequently to see how the house was progressing. We got there by riding the "P" streetcar, which went down Broadway and then to Pico. Although it took only 10-15 minutes to get there, it seemed to Lillie and me that the new house was way out in the country. The street seemed so quiet compared to Olive Street. Watching the house grow was the most exciting thing that had ever happened to us, and Papa was like a child with a new toy. On one red-letter day, Papa took us to the second floor and showed us our bedroom, which overlooked what would be the garden in the back. Mama rarely came with us because it was difficult even for us to get around the construction site. But one Sunday, when the house was almost completed, she came with us and sat in the roof garden as we toured the rooms. Lillie and I decided we wanted something to eat and wheedled some money from her. We made the first of what was to be

Tom Leung in his Pico office.

countless trips to the corner grocery store owned by the Wallace brothers, a couple of taciturn elderly bachelors. It was a dark, musty place. The main attraction for us was the candy counter with its display of all-day suckers, licorice whips, peppermint balls, and all sorts of tempting candies that could be bought for a penny. We were to become some of the Wallace brothers' best customers. We bought bread there daily, as well as other staples, and we children were always running to the corner store to buy penny candies. There was a cash drawer in the desk in our first-floor parlor to which we helped ourselves. Our parents did not supervise the amount of candy we ate. Another place that benefited greatly from our patronage was Carroll's drug store, which was across the street from Wallace's on the corner of Pico and Union. You could get a small ice cream soda for five cents and a big one for ten cents at the long soda fountain. This store was bright and clean. No doubt the businesses in the neighborhood were glad we moved there.

CHAPTER 16

Furnishing and Moving In

Papa bought all the furnishings for the new house at Barker Brothers, which was then located at Seventh and Broadway. Practically all the furniture for the three floors was new, as well as rugs, curtains, and linens. Papa made most of the selections himself, and he bought only the best; he was not a bargain hunter. But he went over the bills carefully, making notations in Chinese. We have pages and pages of bills listing the purchases. Since Mama never went shopping, she left all the decisions to Papa. As with the house plans, he knew exactly what he wanted in furnishings.

For example, on one day, December 6, 1913, he made purchases totalling $437.60 according to a Barker Brothers bill. They included the most expensive pieces of furniture in the house, his big, brown leather chair, $95, and Mama's red, morocco leather chair, $75. Other purchases that day were a dozen assorted chairs, including rocking chairs and a reed "steamer" chair, several tables, a child's iron bed with mattress and springs, a three-foot brass bed, large- and medium-size clothes hampers, and a five-foot step ladder. Compared with today's prices, all this furniture was practically given away. The mahogany dining table, which could be extended to comfortably seat our big family and many guests on festive occasions, cost only $36, and 12 dining room chairs were just $2 each. Papa's satin, brass bed was $30; Mama's mahogany bed, which had a reed inset on the headboard, was $28.50. Her mahogany dresser, a beautifully-crafted piece of furniture, and one of the more expensive selections, cost $78.50. I always loved that dresser; it had an inlay of some other wood for a border and was smooth as silk. Mama kept her clothes folded neatly in the long drawers. In the upper drawers, she had piles of men's handkerchiefs. She always kept one of these tucked into her gown.

The bird's-eye maple bed of which Lillie and I were so proud cost $19.75. The bedroom set included a dresser, $38.50; a chair, $4; and a rocker, $5. Most of this furniture couldn't be bought at thrift store prices today; it was of the best quality. I used some of the $2 dining room chairs until a few years ago. And my favorite chair is a child's mahogany rocker ($5.65) which is still good as new and the most comfortable chair in my living room.

Papa also bought new rugs of well-known make, such as Wilton and Axminister. (The Chinese rugs were not purchased until he went to China in 1921.) Curtains were made to order by Barker Brothers, including velvet portieres ($32) to hang between the hallway and dining room. Linens were all new: 18 sheets for $14, 24 pillow cases for $8, table-cloths, napkins, feather pillows, and comforters. Papa was a thorough shopper. He forgot nothing, even though he never did household chores. Among his miscellaneous purchases were waste baskets, ash trays, a mahogany smoking stand, six cut-glass vases, three dusters, six brooms, three mops, a vacuum cleaner ($35), and two carpet sweepers. These are just some of the pages and pages of items for which he was billed.

The herb room in the new house was, of course, a most important and special place. Papa had Kerton design it like the one at "903." A long counter extended the length of the room on one side and opposite it were two floor-to-ceiling banks of drawers, separated by a sliding door leading to the kitchen. Each drawer contained an herb. There was one herb I loved, called *gum cho*, a yellow, woody disc that had a taste like licorice, but more pungent. Whenever I passed this drawer, I would take a handful to chew on. There were also herbs in big tins on the counter. When Papa finished examining a patient in his office, he would write the prescription and place it through an aperture in the wall near the stairway. Then he would ring a small bell, and the druggist would pick up the prescription and fill it, using the same procedure as was followed at Olive Street. So many doses of herbs were brewed in the kitchen that, after a while, the very walls of the first floor seemed permeated with the pungent, exotic smell of herbs. It greeted you as soon as you walked in the front door. Patients were served their herbs at the dining room table by the receptionist, who at that time was Mabel Johnson.

The day we moved from the "old house" to the "new house" (terms we used for many years) is indelible in my memory. It was January 1, 1914. The Christmas of 1913 was very disappointing to us children. Instead of a big tree that touched the ceiling and piles of gifts around it, there was just a small tree and fewer gifts. Papa was too engrossed in the new house to pay his usual attention to Christmas. There was a touch of sadness, too, that this was our last Christmas in the old house. We had been busy packing and getting ready for weeks. Everything was topsy-turvy, and there was a sign on the lawn announcing the move to "1619" although E Bok Foo still had his office there. Lillie and I had carefully packed all our paper dolls in many boxes and made Mama promise that they would be moved. We went around kissing the walls of the old house in farewell. When the moving van came, we were all beside ourselves with excitement. William cried because he thought the van was taking our belongings where we would never see them again. Papa had gone on to the new house earlier to make things ready, and it was almost dark before the rest of us drove up to "1619" in a cab.

Every light in the house, from basement to roof garden, was ablaze. We children ran from room to room, from floor to floor, delighting in the airy, big rooms, the brand new furniture, the fresh paint smell, and the warmth from the steam radiators. From that first evening, "1619" enveloped us with a love and security I have never felt in any other home. Papa sent Lillie and me across the street to Carroll's drug store to buy some necessities. Mr. Carroll said, "Are you from the family moving into the new house?" We felt proud and important. We knew our house was the biggest and most splendid on the block. The neighborhood hostility that was reported in the beginning seemed to have evaporated. That first night Lillie and I slept on the floor because our bed had not been delivered.

Papa and Mama each had a big bedroom with a sitting room between where they read at night — Papa in his big leather chair and Mama in her red one — before bedtime. Taft and William shared the bedroom across the hall from Lillie's and mine; Howard, Monroe, and Holly had the screen porch and the inside bedroom. The white-tiled bathroom had a big clawfoot tub, a small foot tub which was the little children's bath, and a large sink. Papa had a sink in his bedroom, which he and Mama used. The two third-floor bedrooms and bath were occupied by relatives, at that time, Chuck Ga Sook and Yum Go.

A great disappointment to Lillie and me was the loss of our beloved paper dolls. Somehow (was it planned?) those boxes of dolls never arrived with our other belongings. We had made such a mess of Mama's closet in the old house that perhaps she and Papa decided they were not to be moved. Mama denied this when we asked what had happened. We tried to replenish our supply of paper dolls, but there were other things to do at "1619."

Having to leave Grand Avenue School and transfer to Tenth Street School was a traumatic experience for me. I dreaded the change. The first day the boy next door, whose name I don't recall, walked me to school. It seemed like a long walk compared to the walk to Grand Avenue. I was too shy to talk or play with anyone and sat by myself in the sandpile. Some of the little girls tried to be friendly, but it was some time before I thawed out. I missed my old pal Bessie Bergman at Grand Avenue. The first day I almost got lost going home, running as fast as I could, I was so anxious to get there. I got panicky when I didn't recognize any landmarks. The streets were so quiet and deserted, so different from the busy streets near Grand Avenue School. When a lady came up the street, I asked her where 1619 W. Pico was. She pointed out how I should go, and I finally got home, breathless and relieved. The next day, I let the boy next door walk me home; he did it despite the kidding from the other boys that he had "a girl." His father had tuberculosis and used to lie, very emaciated, on a bed in the screen porch in back. When he died, the family moved.

Lillie didn't attend Tenth Street School. She had started first grade when she was five and had skipped grades. Since there was no junior high then, she went straight to Los Angeles High School, graduating when she was only 16.

It was at Tenth Street that we changed our surname from Tom to Leung because Papa decided it was easier that way. His name in English was Tom Leung (the family name comes first in China), and school authorities couldn't understand why we children went by the surname of Tom rather than Leung. Papa got tired of trying to explain. I had been known as Mamie Tom at Grand Avenue, but when I changed schools, the same old questions were asked, so Papa just had us register as Leung, and I became Mamie Leung. I regret this expedient change, abandoning our true surname.

After a while, I adjusted to the new school. Everyone was friendly. Miss Wallace, the principal, was especially interested in our whole family. Almost every year she'd get a new Leung in the school, and she would show us off to visitors. We'd be called out of class to meet them. We were the only Asians in the school, and she was proud of us. We were good students, docile and obedient.

Jennie Jones, my kindergarten teacher who had become music director of the Los Angeles City School District, started a school orchestra at Tenth Street after I transferred there. I played violin as I had at Grand Avenue, and also continued in the Los Angeles Junior Orchestra. I enjoyed the latter very much. We gave concerts all over the city, always ending with a number called "Boys and Girls of California," which brought rousing applause.

West Pico home library.

A bedroom setting in the West Pico home.

CHAPTER 17

Early Days at Pico

The basement at "1619" was divided into three rooms — the furnace room, the herb storage room, and a big playroom. The laundry tub was in the playroom. A chute led from the second floor to the basement adjacent to the tub. We threw soiled clothing and linens down the chute, and they landed in a big basket. Mary, the maid who had worked at Olive Street, came to "1619." Every morning, she did a big load of laundry, scrubbing on the washboard; then she had to carry it up the basement stairs and outside to the clotheslines. She also made the beds, dusted, and swept the second-floor rooms. The receptionist was responsible for sweeping and dusting Papa's office and the living and dining rooms. In the afternoon, Mary took care of the little children. Sometimes, she would take them to a little park at Alvarado Terrace, and I would go along. There were lovely, big homes surrounding the park; it was an exclusive neighborhood then. Mary would pile the youngest ones into a big wicker buggy, and the rest of us would walk with her the few blocks to the park. Mary liked to tell stories. One of her favorites was a ghost story about a girl in white who wandered every night through the grounds of a large estate wailing "who-o" in an eerie voice. Mary told this so graphically that it frightened me for years, especially when I would lie awake at night. Mary was the most intelligent of the maids and the most devoted to us.

At first, there was a sandbox in the basement, where we played for hours. Eventually, cats somehow got into the sand and dirtied it, so it had to be removed. The cool basement was an especially pleasant place to play on hot summer days. There was a slide which was a favorite pastime; we slid down in twos and threes, slid backwards, and played follow the leader. There was also a cement slide leading from the outside into the herb storage room. Its purpose was to facilitate the transfer of heavy boxes of herbs into the storage room, without having to use the steep, basement steps. We soon discovered that this cement slide was a wonderful place to play despite the wear and tear on our clothes. Later, after we had outgrown the slides, we got a ping-pong table.

The basement also became the den of punishment. When the kids misbehaved — and it had to be something pretty bad — Papa or Mama would order: *"Jick huck her* basement (go immediately to the basement)." The culprit would slink down the stairs; after a while, after our parents' ire had subsided, he would creep back up and insert himself into the family life with as little notice as possible. Neither Lillie nor I ever suffered this banishment. The worst punishment I ever received was when I once played the piano too loudly while Papa was seeing a patient in his office. After the patient left, Papa, without a word, gave me a good whacking with a stick. I will never forget my humiliation. Mama never resorted to corporal punishment, but when she got really angry, her eyes would blaze, and she would shout so loudly at the wrongdoer that he would cringe at her wrath.

William received the worst punishment of all, when he was four years old. He, with Taft, Howard, and Holly, was playing in the library. While Mary, the nurse, was out of the room for a minute, William got hold of a match and ignited a wastebasket full of papers. Mary returned just in time. She rushed to the intercom phone system and called the first floor. (The intercom phones were Papa's idea — there were three on the first floor, one on the second, and one on the third. We children had great fun with these phones at first, but soon tired of this. The only time they really paid off was in this fire crisis.) Lillie, Mabel Johnson and I were having our usual afternoon snack of coffee and crackers in the kitchen. Mabel called the fire department, which responded immediately. Luckily, the kids had jumped over the waste basket soon after the fire started and were not hurt. The blaze was extinguished with little damage, but Papa took William to the roof garden and gave him a hard spanking with a cane. Papa was terribly angry. All the commotion frightened Mama, who was in bed, having recently given birth to Monroe (it was in April, 1915). Mrs. Sylvester, the nurse who always took care of the new babies, was there. The beating he received must have chastened William, who had been the most daring and mischievous of all the kids; he became the most responsible member of the family.

I began playing with Taft more than with Lillie. She had so much to do for Papa and Mama and didn't care much about playing. Taft had a big tricycle, and I used to ride on the back of it. He also made "scooters," boards on wheels, for himself, William, and Howard. None of us ever had a bicycle; we never asked for one, and our parents would probably have refused, thinking it unsafe for us to ride on the street. I don't think we ever had skates either. In comparison with kids of today, we were most unadventurous, but we had fun and always had plenty to do. We were inveterate movie goers. There were two movie theaters nearby. The Sun was a couple of blocks away (near Valencia), and the Empire was a couple of blocks the other way (near Alvarado). Almost every Saturday or Sunday afternoon — sometimes both days — we went to the movies, no matter what was showing. It was the time of silent movies; at the Sun, a piano player provided the accompanying music, and at the Empire, a grander place, there was an organ. Tickets were 10 cents for a whole afternoon's entertainment. There were serials — one called the "Perils of Pauline" — on which we got "hooked," and had to go each week to see the next sequence. Papa enjoyed the movies, too, and he would go at night, taking one of the boys with him. He liked newsreels, but best of all he liked to go downtown to the

The family on the roof patio at the West Pico house.

Orpheum to see vaudeville. Monroe remembers going with him, and when pretty girls came on stage to dance and sing, Papa would take him by the hand and move to a seat closer to the stage. Papa had an eye for pretty women. He had pictures of Mary Pickford and Lillian Gish, reigning favorites of the day, on the wall of the *hoong fong* at Olive Street. After we moved to "1619," Mama never went to the theater with Papa as she had previously, and she had no interest in the movies.

Long before we moved to "1619," automobiles were becoming more and more popular. The day of the horse and buggy was gone. Papa rented a car on Sundays, and we'd all go for a ride. A Mr. Crump was the driver. These drives started at Olive Street. Papa liked to drive around nice residential districts, to the parks, or the beach. Mama didn't care much about cars, but she usually went along. On my very first ride, when I was quite young, I got carsick but didn't mention it. Finally, I threw up but no one noticed till we got home, and I got out of the car. I felt very ashamed. Once, much later on, we drove to Topanga, but the road was so rough and it was so hot and dusty that Papa told

View of the second home, 1619 West Pico.

Crump to turn right around and go back. If Papa had seen
Topanga in the springtime, perhaps he would have liked it as a
place to visit and "get the good air," as he used to say in Chinese.

Papa liked the beach and even the amusement pier, though he
never went on the rides. On one July 3, he took Taft, William,
Howard, and me to an Ocean Park Hotel where we stayed overnight. I was at the age when I loved the amusement pier more
than anything and was excited at spending the entire Fourth of
July there. Papa didn't stay with us that day — he left me in
charge and picked us up in the evening. The pier was so crowded
it was hard to get on the rides. I didn't have as good a time as I
had anticipated, but staying overnight in the beach hotel was
memorable.

CHAPTER 18

From Gee Sook to Beatty

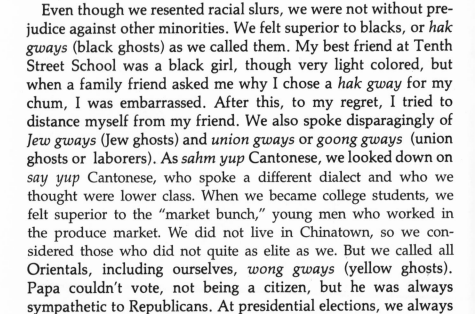

Even though we resented racial slurs, we were not without prejudice against other minorities. We felt superior to blacks, or *hak gways* (black ghosts) as we called them. My best friend at Tenth Street School was a black girl, though very light colored, but when a family friend asked me why I chose a *hak gway* for my chum, I was embarrassed. After this, to my regret, I tried to distance myself from my friend. We also spoke disparagingly of *Jew gways* (Jew ghosts) and *union gways* or *goong gways* (union ghosts or laborers). As *sahm yup* Cantonese, we looked down on *say yup* Cantonese, who spoke a different dialect and who we thought were lower class. When we became college students, we felt superior to the "market bunch," young men who worked in the produce market. We did not live in Chinatown, so we considered those who did not quite as elite as we. But we called all Orientals, including ourselves, *wong gways* (yellow ghosts). Papa couldn't vote, not being a citizen, but he was always sympathetic to Republicans. At presidential elections, we always supported the Republican candidate. The Democratic Party, in our opinion, was the party of poor people or *goong gways,* so we sided with the Republicans. However, we were more or less apolitical. It wasn't until after I had graduated from college and was working that I cast my first vote — as a Democrat. Mama had no interest in what went on in the American political scene, but she was an avid reader of Chinese newspapers. Perhaps one reason we grew up with this snobbish attitude was because we had a cook, a maid, and a nurse, and we noticed that most people didn't. We were proud that our father was the most successful herbalist in Los Angeles, and that he was highly respected by the Chinese community. Yet our parents did not foster these opinions. Perhaps it was our life style. Much later, we were to learn what it meant to be poor.

The move to "1619," where Papa set up business under the name of T. Leung Herb Co., and the breakup of the partnership with E Bok Foo, were causes for rancor. In fact, E Bok Foo was very angry. When Papa first broached the subject of moving to a bigger house, there were angry discussions. E Bok Foo spent much time in his offices in Oakland and Boston. When he returned to Los Angeles, he wanted to move into "1619." He wanted control of the herb business there. Papa was willing to share fifty-fifty, but E Bok Foo insisted he should have half interest in the house also. He ordered Papa to get out of the herb business and leave the city. One night, the argument got so heated that E Bok Foo threw a flower pot at Papa, who left the room. E Bok Foo probably reasoned that he had invited Papa to come to this country in the first place and had taught him the herb business. He moved into "1619," and Mama gave him her room. He worked and ate at Olive street and came to "1619" to sleep. Papa and Mama kept their bedroom door shut, and E Bok Foo stayed in his room. The second floor "parlor" was unused. This uncomfortable situation went on for two or three months, when E Bok Foo finally went back to "903," but the family squabble was never settled, and E Bok Foo and Papa were no longer partners, but competitors.

Gee Sook, our cook who had been with us so long at Olive street, came with us to "1619." He continued to live in Chinatown, arriving early each morning on the "P" streetcar. We children had by this time given up eating *jook* (rice gruel) for breakfast. Sometimes we had cornflakes, but more often than not we would go to school without breakfast. Our parents began eating oatmeal for breakfast, which Mama cooked. At Olive Street, Gee Sook had made sandwiches for Lillie and me for our school lunch, but he cut the bread so thick that we were ashamed to eat in front of the other children and began making our own lunches. In the early afternoon, Gee Sook took his straw basket, boarded the "P" car, and went to Chinatown to shop for our evening meal, just as he had done at Olive street. He used the wood stove, winter or summer. He sat at the top of the basement steps and ate. He never felt quite at home in the new house. Papa insisted that the white-tile kitchen floor be mopped daily and that the stoves and counters be kept clean. After a year or two, he told Papa he was going back to China, that he was getting old and wanted to die there. He had saved enough money from his small earnings to buy a ticket home to Canton. His departure was a blow to our parents. They wanted to continue eating Chinese meals as they had since they'd left China, and they tried in vain to find a replacement for Gee Sook. Finally they gave up this quest and hired a *hak gway* cook named Beatty from an employment agency. She turned out to be a Southern cook of gourmet quality. Since I didn't like Chinese food, I was ecstatic.

The first breakfast Beatty cooked still stands out in my memory. It was served, fittingly, in the breakfast room, an airy, light room that opened onto the back garden. The chilled melon was cut with scalloped edges, the eggs were scrambled just right, and I had never tasted such fluffy, delicious biscuits. Even Mama ate a whole biscuit. Beatty had certain specialties, such as oxtail soup and fried sand-dabs, which were Papa's favorite. Mama, whose taste for American food was lukewarm, genuinely liked not only Beatty's biscuits, but her spoonbread. She jealously guarded her recipes, and long after she had left, we tried in vain to duplicate her spoonbread. The Johnson sisters found her strawberry shortcake especially mouth-watering. They tried to wheedle and bribe the recipe from Beatty, who shut herself into the pantry when she stirred up the batter. I gorged on the meals, gaining weight. But our parents still yearned for their Chinese food. On Beatty's day off, Mama tried her hand at cooking. She had watched Gee Sook and had picked up some rudiments of Chinese cooking — things she had never learned during her pampered girlhood. Eventually she became a good cook and knew how to make Papa's favorite dishes. She taught Lillie, too, and later, Holly; they both became excellent cooks — American and Chinese style — but in the kitchen I was known as *lun jun* or clumsy and slow.

The garden at the back of the new house was laid out in formal style, according to Papa's plan. There was a fountain in the middle and a summerhouse in the back. Gravel paths divided the planting plots. Two plots in front were planted in grass. Papa ordered all the trees, flowers, and shrubs from his old friend and teacher Paul Howard of the Howard and Smith Nursery, which was on its way to becoming one of the most successful nurseries in Los Angeles. The nursery also did the soil preparation and planting at the cost of $3.50 per day per man. At that time, the plantings were practically given away. We have a bill dated March 31, 1914, for $140.33 which covered all the original landscaping — labor included. Among the plantings listed are bay and rubber trees, bamboo, 18 varieties of shrubs, 100 dusty millers, phlox, ficus, 24 petunias, 50 calla lillies, jasmine, magnolia, a dozen hanging baskets, and roses (including two climbing Cecil Brunners). I remember the latter well because they bloomed so profusely, almost covering the summer house with tiny pink roses. The garden was enclosed by a decorative, white fence, high enough to insure complete privacy, not only from neighbors, but also from the utility part of our yard where the woodshed and clothesline were. Since the plants were mature, not seedlings, the garden soon was a pleasure to enjoy. Papa installed lights for nighttime enjoyment.

Monroe's lively document about the family (written about 1940) describes Papa's love of his garden:

Every morning before going to his office, he would smoke his water pipe in the back porch (which overlooked the garden) and look at his plants, especially the ones lining the porch rails and stone steps. This is one *definite habit* I will always remember he did. On rainy days he'd merely stand by the screen door of the breakfast room and peer out. He did this before and immediately after his breakfast which was at about 10 a.m. When he came home at night he would do the same. One night he noticed a pair of cat's eyes in the dark and seemed very interested. He described them as being like *two lanterns*. Whenever there was a full moon he used to keep the garden lights closed and admire the moonlight. He admired the moonlight just like I do now. Dad kept up an endless vigil against scraps of paper and leaves on the ground and always made us pick them up. My dad was *always neat*.

Mama also smoked a water pipe, but not outdoors. When she woke in the morning, she would take her first smoke in the bathroom, sitting on the stool by the toilet. After she came downstairs, she smoked two or three times a day — always sitting in the chair by the kitchen stove. For a while, it was my job to clean these water pipes, a smelly job that I intensely disliked. Mama also smoked cigarettes. She had started smoking them when she was a young girl, but she told Myra Lee, "I don't want my girls to smoke." We never did. Papa never smoked cigarettes; he smoked cigars and a pipe. He was particular about what he smoked and patronized an exclusive place called John's Pipe Shop in downtown Los Angeles. Their delivery wagon made frequent trips to our home; it was in the form of a large pipe drawn by a pony. Papa always bought the best in tobacco, imported mixtures, and a brand called Long Cut Tobacco which he and Mama used in their water pipes. He kept the tobacco in a jar with a lettuce leaf over it to keep it fresh and moist. His favorite pipe was made in Ireland. When we were very young, Lillie and I loved the fancy paper rings that came around the cigars, and later, we vied for the wooden cigar boxes in which to keep our treasures. The cigar smell clung to them no matter how long we kept them.

Monroe was correct in stating that Papa was neat. Papa had Mabel type up these instructions for the maid:

All the floors must be swept with a broom once a week;
the first floor on Friday, the second floor on Saturday,
and the third floor on Tuesday.
Scrub the bathrooms on the first and third floors twice a
week.
Scrub bathroom on second floor every day.
Sweep the steps twice a week, and dust them every day.
In the kitchen clean the stoves, icebox, woodwork, etc.,
every Thursday.
Use the hose on the front and back porches on Tuesday
and Saturday. Sweep them every day.
If the rooms are not very dirty, they need not be swept,
but only dusted and mopped, except the children's
rooms, which must be swept every day.
Sweep the roof garden once a week.

Since the maid also had to do the huge daily washings and look after the young children, she had her hands full. However, I doubt that the instructions were followed to the letter because the maids seemed to have plenty of time to take us to the parks or to the movies in the afternoons.

Originally, the front porch extended the width of the house; but Papa soon decided that his office was too cramped and small, so he had about a third of the porch glassed in, doubling his office space and still leaving plenty of porch. He was always making improvements. After Gee Sook left, there was no need for the woodshed so that was torn down. (There was no need for the wood stove either, but it was built into the kitchen and too difficult to remove.) A structure was built at the back of the utility section of the yard. For a short time it was used as a playhouse but soon became living quarters for students. One was C.C. Lee, a silent young man, who gave us Chinese lessons. There were steps leading from this structure to the flat roof where the clotheslines were placed. This made even more work for the maid, who had to bring the wet laundry up the steep basement stairs, outdoors to the yard, and then up the steps to the clotheslines. Lillie and I learned how difficult this was when we did the laundry, though our task was much easier. By that time, we had a wringer-type washing machine which was on the back porch; we had to carry the clothes basket up only one flight of stairs, but we complained bitterly.

Sometimes Papa would have his morning smoke on the second floor balcony, which extended the width of the house; the sitting room and Mama's bedroom opened onto this balcony. Chinese ceramic pots planted with flowers in season were displayed on the wide shelf atop the balcony railing. On warm evenings the whole family would sit out there. The view here — of traffic on Pico Street — was less than desirable. For some reason, we seldom made use of the roof garden, where there was the most privacy and quiet and a comfortable lawn swing. Here again, Papa had potted plants. In the fall, the chrysanthemums were a riot of color. The petals were used in a fish dish that Papa liked. The Fourth of July was one time when we would gather on the roof garden, to watch the fireworks display from Exposition Park.

CHINESE AMERICANS

CHAPTER 19

The World's Fair

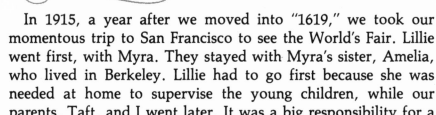

In 1915, a year after we moved into "1619," we took our momentous trip to San Francisco to see the World's Fair. Lillie went first, with Myra. They stayed with Myra's sister, Amelia, who lived in Berkeley. Lillie had to go first because she was needed at home to supervise the young children, while our parents, Taft, and I went later. It was a big responsibility for a 13-year-old, especially since Monroe was an infant of only a few months. We had been preparing for months for this vacation. I had a lot of new clothes. Mama made me a white, serge dress with lavender piping, of which I was very proud. Myra, an expert seamstress, made me a party dress of white Chinese silk with pink rosebuds around the neck and waist. Mama wore her American dresses and her custom-made high button shoes that were so uncomfortable. She took the white fox fur Papa had bought her, and, of course, the one-karat diamond earrings she always wore. Papa bought her many pieces of valuable jewelry, which she seldom wore, but she took a few of these with her, as well as a bottle of the perfume he liked. He used to order samples from

New York, and then buy the ones he favored. Usually, the scents were too strong for Mama's liking. She preferred Florida water and used it all her life. I like to have a bottle of it around because it reminds me of her.

We went to San Francisco by boat. To get to San Pedro harbor, we took a cab to the Pacific Electric station, and rode the Red Car to the pier. Papa tipped the cab driver a dollar — at that time a rashly generous tip, but Papa was feeling in great, good humor that day. I was a little fearful of getting seasick, but the first day at sea was beautiful and calm. Taft and I had a wonderful time exploring the big vessel, running up and down the stairs to the different decks, and peeking into the lounges and dining rooms. We had a spacious stateroom. Papa walked with us part of the time, but Mama enjoyed just sitting in a deck chair. The meals were lavish and excellent. At night, we watched the dancing in the ballroom. At that time, there were two ways of getting to San Francisco, by boat or by train; I decided that nothing could be more pleasant than the boat. The next morning I woke up feeling strange. I didn't want to eat breakfast but went to the dining room with the others anyway. The smell of bacon and eggs was sickening. When the hot chocolate I had ordered was served with a big dollop of whipped cream floating on top, I knew I had to get out of there quickly and made Mama go with me. Of course, she couldn't walk fast, and we barely made it to the deck when I vomited. I felt horrible. Some men who saw me laughed, and that really humiliated me. When we got to our stateroom, I cried; I had never been so miserable before, and was afraid I'd vomit again. The ocean entering the Golden Gate was rougher than anything Mama had experienced on her month-long trip from China. Mama tried to comfort me; she was so solicitous and good. She said we would soon be in San Francisco. I felt especially bad because Taft wasn't sick and was having a good time. "I won't take the boat home," I wailed, knowing we had round-trip tickets. "I'll never get on a boat again." We arrived in San Francisco about noon. As soon as we got off the rocking ship, I felt less nauseous. We went directly to the fairgrounds and to the hotel there, called the Inside Inn. We had two rooms with a connecting bath. I was still weak and sick so I was put to bed for a nap. When I awoke, I felt fine, and we went to the dining room for dinner. My appetite had returned, and I ate ravenously. The hotel was brand new and luxurious. Waiters seemed to sense that Papa was a good tipper so we got the best service.

The Fair's theme building was the Tower of Jewels. It looked spectacular all lit up at night. Papa got a picture of it which hung in our second-floor living room for a long time. Taft and I liked the food exhibits best. There was a building where you could get enough free samples for a meal. We collected literature everywhere. Papa spent a lot of time in the Fine Arts building, which we found boring. He spent hours looking at the pictures by famous artists. Mama couldn't walk around with the rest of us, but it was possible to hire a man to push you around the fairgrounds in chairs, and Papa and Mama rode these. Much of the time, Mama would sit on a bench and wait for us. The Japanese exhibit included a tearoom where we had tea and rice cakes. It was convenient living on the fairgrounds in a fine hotel. I enjoyed it immensely and was sorry when we left after about a week. We stayed one night in a hotel in San Francisco Chinatown operated by Chinese. Papa wanted to try it, but what a change from the spotless, modern Inside Inn! It was so dirty that Mama was sure there were bedbugs. I had a room to myself, and Mama advised me to lock the door and keep the key in it. The next morning we moved out.

Someone suggested the Sutter Hotel because it was on Grant Avenue close enough to Chinatown so Mama could walk. Papa had many friends in Chinatown so we went there every day for the balance of our visit. Taft and I found this boring, but we collected a lot of *lai see*. It's the custom to give a child *lai see* the first time you see him. My purse was stuffed with money wrapped in red paper. Papa seemed to know the owners of all the stores along Grant Avenue. The one place I liked visiting was the jewelry store. I watched the men sitting at wooden tables, pounding gold into shape, and using delicate tongs to place insets of jade and pearl into the soft metal. Once we visited an apartment where a woman was having her hair fixed in Chinese style. The long, black hair was carefully combed and brushed, plastered with a thick, gooey mixture, and then coiled in the back in a shiny bun which was decorated with jade pins. Every gleaming hair was in place. The women in Chinatown wore pants and jackets, and many had bound feet. Mama felt at home there — it reminded her of China. Everyone spoke Chinese; they knew little, if any, English. When they discovered Taft and I spoke no Chinese, they were amazed. "They're Chinese and can't speak Chinese," they exclaimed, making us feel ashamed. I also felt resentful at their attitude. I saw no reason then why I should speak Chinese since I lived in America. But our parents were defensive. "They're learning Chinese," they said. "They're taking lessons." I could see our American ways were an embarrassment to them. They especially liked Chinatown because of the good restaurants; their favorites were Peking Low and Shanghai Low. This was where I had my first taste of Peking duck, which my parents called *gwa lo op*, and which was unobtainable in Los Angeles. I liked it but still thought longingly of the American meals at the Inside Inn. Chinatown didn't appeal to me; I thought it was dirty and smelly. The stores were dark, and people were crowded into small rooms.

All during the trip, Mama worried about the children at home, especially Monroe, who was just an infant. After a week at the Sutter, she was anxious to get home. I had been insisting all along that I wouldn't take the boat home — I was terrified of getting seasick again. So, since Mama was eager to get home as soon as possible, and the train was the quickest way, Papa cancelled the return trip by boat. Trains then were much more pleasant than they are now; we took the Lark, which was the best of all and the fastest. We had a compartment. Taft and I had the upper berth and enjoyed the novelty of sleeping on the train as well as eating in the immaculate, well-appointed dining car. At home, things were fine. Lillie had done her usual good job. Of course, she had not been left alone with the children. Chuck Ga Sook and Yum Go lived on the third floor, and Mary came every day, but the main responsibility for the children was Lillie's.

That same year, 1915, there also was a world's fair in San Diego. After we returned from San Francisco, Papa opened a branch of the herb company in San Diego and placed Chuck Ga Sook in charge. Papa took Taft and me to see the fair and, also, to check on the office. This fair was much smaller than the one in San Francisco, and I remember nothing about it. We spent most of our time in the branch office, which was located in a small house in a residential district near downtown. Taft and I preferred staying in our hotel, the U.S. Grant — riding up and down in the elevators and talking to the bellboys. At night, we sat on the hotel balcony where you could see the lights of the city. We made more than one trip to San Diego. Once, we stayed at the Hotel del Coronado. Mama went with us that time, to *tahn* (take it easy). I always liked going places with Papa because he chose the best. On trips, he never rode street cars but took cabs no matter how short the distance. The San Diego office didn't do well. Chuck lacked Papa's personality and ability to deal with people. There were other small branch offices in Redlands and Riverside where Papa would hold office hours. He also had an extensive mail order business in Canada. Wells Fargo was in the parcel post business then, and several times a week, its vehicle would stop at our house to pick up packages of herbs destined for Canada. How Papa got this mail order business, I don't know, but it proved a mainstay in lean times to come.

There was an herb order blank which each patient who came to the office was asked to fill out. The form contained questions such as these: "How often do your bowels move? How often do you pass urine during 24 hours? What is its color? Is there any pain in passing urine? Is your appetite good? Do you sleep well? Have you pains in the head? Have you any cough, any phlegm? Have you asthma? Rheumatism? Syphilitic poison? Dysentery? Eczema?" There was also space for "general remarks." It concluded: "We will make a thorough study of these answers, and we will send the proper remedies by express or mail, changing the herbs every other week, or perhaps every three weeks, when that plan seems to be better." Similar blanks were sent to the patients in Canada, and on the basis of the answers they were treated, sight unseen.

Apparently, many of the patients in Canada were satisfied with their treatment. Whenever they got sick, they sent for herbal remedies. Even though they never saw Papa, they remained his patients through the years.

Papa's booklet *Chinese Herbal Science* contains many glowing testimonials from grateful patrons who said they were cured by herbs. The letters, many of them notarized, seem too sincere to be fabricated. All are signed with names and addresses, some of which I recognize. Here is an excerpt from one especially long letter dated February 26, 1918 (this man had a friend who had recommended him to go to Papa for a longtime illness):

I told my friend if all the good AMERICAN doctors which I have had can't cure me, there is NO USE going to a CHINK. I said this because I was IGNORANT of the thorough and scientific education of the CHINESE HERBALISTS, and because of the PREJUDICE and EGOTISM we AMERICANS have against any other than the white race. I was now in terrible condition. The doctors had given me up ... As it was my only hope, I put aside my prejudice and went. The first time T. Leung saw me I told him my symptoms and he said, "You have stomach trouble ... You are so near dead that I do not know whether my medicine will get a hold on you before your heart stops. If it does, our herbs will help you." ... To make a long story short, it has now been three years since I stopped taking the herbs, and I am a pretty fine specimen of health, and a good advertisement proclaiming the scientific herbal skill of T. Leung. I will be glad to answer any inquiries that may come to me, at my address ...

CHAPTER 20

1918

Although Papa had designed "1619" to be his office as well as our family home, he found that business was not as good as it had been at Olive Street. Pico Street was too far from downtown; people found it inconvenient, so he established an office in a big storefront building at 711 S. Main St. (though he still kept office hours at "1619" for those who preferred to go there). The Main Street office was a success from the start. It was in the midst of downtown with heavy street traffic. A big sign over the entrance said: "T. Leung Herb Co. Under the Same Manager in this City since 1896. Pure Natural Herb Remedies Good for All Ailments." The spacious waiting room was furnished with deep sofas and comfortable chairs. Patients drank their herbs at small round tables in a white-latticed bower trimmed with artificial pink roses. To my child's eyes, this was really beautiful. Papa's private office was furnished with a large, polished mahogany desk. Bookcases held volumes on Chinese herbal medicine. There were also an herb room, kitchen, and bedroom where Chuck Ga Sook or the druggist slept. A big, glass display window was neatly

T. Leung Herb Co. at 711 South Main.

arranged with an exhibit of herbs and Chinese art to attract the passersby. The receptionist at that time was Willa, the daughter of Elva Brooker, who had been Lillie's nurse. Willa was exceptionally good in talking with patients, Papa said; she helped to stimulate and initiate business. Papa earned $4,000 a month at Main street, a good sum of money in those days. Willa couldn't type, so Lillie had to go to the store every day to type letters.

World War I didn't affect us much. There was rationing of certain foods, and we ate a lot of cornbread, which was a favorite with Mama. Lillie and I knit scarfs out of khaki yarn for the soldiers. Actually, we knew only one soldier, Willie Yip. Toward the end of the war, when manpower was growing short, Papa had to register for the draft. Lillie went with him to Sentous Junior High to sign up. We considered this a joke because Papa, with a family of eight children, would never be called. Nor could we imagine Papa as a soldier. It was just unthinkable. On November 11, 1918, I was in class at Sentous Junior High when it was announced that the war was over. The armistice had been declared. School was dismissed, and we all rushed home. Papa phoned from the office and told us to call a cab and come down there. We were all in a state of high excitement, even Mama. When we got to 711 S. Main Street, in the midst of downtown, the streets were already thronged with cars and people, shouting, singing, crying, jubilant that the "war to end all wars" had ended. It was a wild, happy, hysterical scene. Strangers hugged each other. The office was full of people. We phoned friends to join us. Papa kept sending out for food. The celebration went on far into the night. How disappointing that we took no pictures of that wonderful day.

Our parents never relaxed in their determination that we children learn to speak, read and write Chinese. They saw us becoming more and more American, surrounded everywhere by Western influence. From time to time, they would issue an ultimatum that we must speak only Chinese at home. This would last only a few days, and then we would lapse back into English or pidgin Chinese when we talked to Mama. The "Chinese only" ultimatum didn't work because none of us knew enough Chinese to communicate effectively. We had a long succession of tutors. When Papa saw that the lessons during summer vacation weren't sufficient, he hired teachers to come at night, during the school term. Lillie and I were taught in the library by a stout, easy-going man who allowed me to continue my habit of writing the American phonetic sound beside the Chinese characters. Periodically, Papa would hold tests, calling us into the upstairs parlor one by one. I knew I couldn't remember the lessons without the phonetics, so I would go into the bathroom just before my turn came. Papa would call someone else and forget about me. No one else in the family complained about these Chinese lessons like I did. Yet, I was very good in Latin and French.

Mary, who had been with us for many years, finally left, and was replaced by Nettie, our last nursemaid. She was a young, married woman with a baby. During summer vacation, I spent every day with her. She took me and the boys to cheap movies on Main Street, really "junky" stuff about white slavery, etc. Once a man followed us when we left the movie. Nettie was frightened, and we walked as fast as we could to Papa's office at Seventh and

Main. Nettie didn't take us to parks, as Mary had, but she did share my enthusiasm for the Venice pier. Two or three times a summer, taking only Monroe, we would walk to Venice Boulevard and take the Red Car directly to the beach. Mama gave me $2, which was all we needed for a day. We went on all the rides, including the ghost house and ferris wheel, and lunched on hot dogs and cotton candy. We were both enamored with the "Race Through the Clouds," a roller coaster which we rode as many as eight times in succession, leaving Monroe in the ticket booth with the cashier. Once we took Monroe, who was only about two, on a ride called the "Whip," and he was so frightened that he cried. He liked the merry-go-round, but that was too tame for us. It was Nettie who told me the "facts of life" and in such a crude way that I was horrified. I didn't believe her. If our parents had known what Nettie was telling me, they would have gotten rid of her immediately. When she left to have another baby, I missed her. She was as much a child as I; now I had no one to play jacks with or to take me to the pier.

Mincie was the last of Mama's nine children. He was born in the spring of 1917. That night, Holly and the boys had gone to sleep in their rooms. Lillie and I were doing our homework in the office. Papa was lying on the office sofa, arms folded behind his head, staring at the ceiling. He was obviously worried. Mama had been in labor for a long time — unusual for her, and there was no sound from her bedroom upstairs except for the occasional scurrying around of Mrs. Mueller, the midwife. Lillie was restless and jumpy, unable to keep her mind on her books. Papa spoke to her sharply: "Why don't you study like Mamie?" Despite Nettie, I was unsure how babies were born, so I was not too concerned. Occasionally, I went into the kitchen where Yum Go was making Chinese sponge cake, which is steamed, not baked, and was one of my favorite confections. Yum Go was always calm and thoughtful, and he made the sponge cake that night as a diversion. It was cooked to perfection. He cut me a big wedge of the light, fluffy *gay don go*; Lillie ate some, but Papa was too preoccupied to eat. Time dragged on. Suddenly, there was a cry from upstairs — the cry of the newborn. Papa smiled and sat up. Lillie and I started to rush upstairs, but Papa said

The palatial reception room at 711 South Main.

to wait awhile. When we finally went into Mama's room, she looked exhausted, pale, and very small in the big bed. Beside her was the bundle of baby. *Ho sun foo* (very much suffering), she told Papa. She was too old to have babies, she said. Papa nodded sympathetically. Lillie and I eagerly plucked aside the blankets to look at the red, wrinkled face of our new baby brother.

It was in the next year, 1918, that the deadly influenza epidemic struck. The illness was so contagious that the schools were closed for a long period. We did assignments at home and sent them to school. People were urged to wear bags of medicine around their necks (the name I forget) which was supposed to ward off the disease. Papa originated an herb prescription that was quite effective against the illness, and cured many flu victims. No one in our family got the disease. But there was sickness and death everywhere. A young couple and their two babies lived in the house next door. We never knew the family. The parents got the flu and died within days. We could see and hear the grandmother sobbing over the babies from our second-floor bathroom which was just opposite one of their bedrooms. This frightened and depressed us all.

The herb room at the T. Leung Co. on 711 South Main.

CHAPTER 21

Music and Tennis

Papa's liking for American music began shortly after he came to this country; he especially liked the cornet. He bought a gold-plated cornet with flower designs and mother-of-pearl key faces. A teacher, who tried valiantly to instruct Papa in the use of this costly instrument, was hired, but the resulting sounds were anything but musical. His inability to play did not deter Papa from joining the Chinese band that was directed by an old man whose real job was running a bicycle repair shop. There were twenty members in the band, including 11-year-old Peter Soo Hoo, who was to marry Lillie. Peter recalled Papa's joining the band in 1911 and how the younger members admired his fine clothes, gold-handled cane, and expensive cornet. The band took part in the Shriners' parade that year despite the fact that their repertoire consisted only of a garbled rendition of Yankee Doodle. They made up for their lack of musical expertise by their resplendent uniforms of long Chinese robes, Chinese leggings and red fezzes. The three-mile line of march began at Tenth and Grand and ended at First and Main; this was too much for Papa, who wasn't used to walking long distances, and he dropped out about half way through. Pete said Lillie and I tagged along with the band. This was only one of several parades at that Shriners' convention, including an electrical one at night. The line of march always passed Grand Avenue, a block from our house. Lillie and I took camp stools and went early in the morning to hold a place for the family. Papa loved parades, and even Mama enjoyed them, though she got tired.

Papa finally gave up his losing battle with the cornet and gave the instrument to Taft, who was immediately more successful. It was Papa's ambition to have a family orchestra like George Lem's, whose children played regularly at church functions and at the Lem restaurant and gained quite a reputation. William was given clarinet lessons and Howard, flute. Monroe played drums, Holly, piano, and Mincie, violin. A lot of money was spent on our lessons and instruments, but none of us practiced seriously. We did play in the school orchestras, but Papa's dream of a family orchestra never materialized. Sometimes when visitors came, they would ask us to play, and we would do so but with much reluctance; since we never practiced together, our performance was substandard. Lillie and I liked to play jazz — the latest hits on sheet music — on the piano. Papa didn't like jazz, but he didn't try to stop us, though on occasion he would walk out of the room with a disgusted remark about *cho gway* (low-class ghost) music. He bought Lillie a grand piano when she graduated from junior high school. I liked playing this much more than my violin. Later on, Lillie and I performed for the Chinese Students Club of the University of Southern California, but my fiddle playing left much to be desired.

At Olive Street we had what was called a "talking machine" with a horn. Papa enjoyed Sousa's band playing military tunes like "Stars and Stripes Forever." The music from the talking machine was loud but scratchy. When we moved to "1619," Papa bought a phonograph which was the state-of-the-art music box of the times. He took Lillie and me with him to a music store to buy a stack of records. We were interested only in jazz and dance tunes, but he refused to listen to any of them. Instead, he bought a bookful of classical records, including violin and cornet solos, and symphonies. Lillie and I were quite disgruntled at his selections. Later, we went alone and bought jazz records. Every evening after dinner, Papa listened to his music until the novelty wore off. It was the first time I had heard Debussy and I learned to like it, as well as the other records. Even now, when I hear these classics, they bring back memories of those evenings in the downstairs parlor listening to the phonograph. The jazz records have long since been forgotten. In Chinatown, Papa bought records of Chinese opera. Mama, who didn't care for American music of any kind, loved those records. Both our parents had a passion for Chinese opera. Whenever an opera troupe came to Chinatown, they would go to every evening performance. The performances would often last till very late at night, but Mama never got tired. Afterwards, she and Papa would discuss the merits and demerits of the actors. She said it reminded her of China. We children thought the opera was grotesque, and abominable — the affected, stilted acting, the singing that was more like screeching, and the ear-splitting din from the shirt-sleeved musicians. Since then, I have seen the Peking opera in China, in more sophisticated settings, but my opinion has not changed. We had Chinese flutes and a Chinese piano which we kept in the library, but no one knew how to play them.

Tennis was a sport Papa admired, and he asked our friend, Frank Frank to teach him. He bought himself the best of racquets and some sporty white tennis togs. The three "big kids" (the way we spoke of Taft, William and Howard) and I went along to the tennis court. The boys' job was to pick up the balls. Frank tried his best to teach Papa, but after a few afternoons it was evident that it was of no avail. Papa was too stout and too clumsy and slow. He also wanted to learn ballroom dancing, and hired an instructor for this purpose. The Johnson sisters had already taught Lillie and me how to dance. We rolled up the rugs and danced to the phonograph. The Johnsons, as well as Myra and Helen Lee, were there when the dancing teacher came. But Papa was no better at dancing than he was at tennis. The rest of us enjoyed dancing with the teacher, who taught us new steps. Papa struggled on, with whatever hapless partner he chose.

Walking was one type of exercise he could handle. Almost

The family in the backyard, mid-1920's.

every night after dinner he took a walk around the block, wearing his hat and carrying his cane. He always took one of the boys with him. Occasionally, none of them were available, so I would have to go. I felt uncomfortable on these walks because they were taken in almost complete silence. I didn't know what to say, and Papa was interested only in walking, though once in a while he would comment on something along the way. Monroe was his favorite walking partner; in fact, we thought Monroe was his favorite child; Papa usually chose him to accompany him on his frequent attendance at movies and vaudeville. "One reason why Pop usually took me places (not because I was father's favorite boy) was because of my height," Monroe wrote in his essay on life at "1619." "He always grabbed or held on to me by the upper part of my left arm, which was sort of a combination arm rest and cane for him. Sometimes he held on so tightly that my blood circulation would stop and he'd immediately let go. He always used to go to the Sunken Gardens at Exposition Park on Sundays. He'd take me (I never enjoyed going) if no other member of the family would go." On one of their walks, Monroe said he got up the courage to ask Papa if he played with his brother, Chuck Ga Sook, when they were young. Papa's answer was a tense: "Do you play with Mincie?" This was about the closest any of us had come to asking Papa about his youth.

CHAPTER 22

Race Prejudice

Mama always maintained there was no romantic love, as we know it, between her and Papa, but they had a mostly harmonious relationship. Mama did everything she could do to please Papa, making his favorite foods, seeing that he was comfortable, and making sure that the children picked up their toys and that the house was neat when he came home. His wants and needs came first with her. Unlike most Chinese husbands, Papa gave her furs and jewels and expensive perfume. He always saw that she had money. When she was in bed after childbirth (the only time she ever took to her bed), he saw to it that she had tea, cigarettes and money on her bedside table. She never went shopping, but she doled out the money for groceries and household needs. Both our parents were avid readers. In the evenings, after Papa's walk, they would go upstairs to the second-floor parlor. Papa sat in his brown leather chair and Mama nearby in her red leather one, and they would read Chinese newspapers and books all evening. They discussed things together. We children never asked Papa directly for anything —

Mama was our intermediary, and it was during those quiet times that she would raise our requests. Papa was indulgent and generous; he opened charge accounts at all the large department stores. Lillie and I used them freely, but he never complained about the bills. I was even charging my clothes in later years after I went to work.

Papa made the decisions and Mama usually agreed with them. Lavender was Papa's favorite color, and Mama wore it, even though she didn't care for it. On more important decisions, she went along with him, too. When Taft was about eight, and William and Howard about six and five, Papa decided they should go to China for a few years and live in a Chinese school in Canton. He was discouraged that none of us were learning Chinese, despite all our lessons, and felt we were becoming too Americanized. Mama wasn't too happy about having her boys go so far away for so long, but she agreed it was the only way they would get a real Chinese education and be exposed to Chinese culture. Papa wrote to relatives and friends about which school would be best for the boys. Meanwhile, he outfitted them with military uniforms to give them a neat and dignified appearance, bought luggage, and even applied for passports. Everything was in readiness for the trip when Papa got a letter from China advising him not to send the boys at that time; the political situation was too unstable and it could be dangerous. I was relieved since I had been dreading their departure; I was afraid they might not return. I hated having the family broken up. The boys themselves hadn't rebelled against the trip; perhaps they even looked forward to it as an adventure. Papa was disappointed. He had even had a family picture taken on the upstairs balcony with the boys in their military regalia. Even Monroe had a uniform, but not as elegant as those of the older boys. Mincie was too young for one. He wore rompers and sat on Papa's lap. (There is a copy of this picture in *Chinese Herbal Science.*)

Since the boys couldn't go to China, Papa wanted to enroll Taft in a military school because he thought the discipline was good. He sent for literature from schools such as the Urban and the Page military academies, which were quite expensive. One Sunday, we visited them and tried to register Taft, but he wasn't accepted because he was Chinese.

About this time, I had my first bad experience with race prejudice. Our class at Sentous Junior High was planning a party; I was excited and planned to go. One of the girls, who I thought was a friend of mine, took me aside and told me I wasn't to come to the party. She didn't say why, nor did she speak in an unfriendly way, but acted as though I should have known I wasn't wanted at the party. I was terribly shocked. Lillie and I had been called "Chink" and "skibee" by strange boys on our way to school, but this was the first time I was directly confronted with the issue of prejudice, and I was unsure how to deal with it. No one else told me I shouldn't go; I thought perhaps the teacher would, but she said nothing. I didn't tell anyone, not even Lillie, what that girl had said. A meeting was held to decide on the details of the party. I decided to attend and offered to take certain responsibilities. I simply ignored what the girl had said, and she did not repeat her warning. I went to the party, but I didn't enjoy it. From then on, I felt race-conscious with my schoolmates. I had always wanted to be like them. I didn't like being different, but now there was something more — shame and anger. These feelings were emphasized in another incident, years later, when I went to the beach on a date. We went to the dance hall at Ocean Park. The man at the ticket booth said, "This dance hall is for whites only." We walked away, humiliated. Instead of venting our anger and talking about the incident, we felt so ashamed we never mentioned it. Of course, we should have seen that it was they, not we, who should be ashamed, but that was long before the civil rights movement. And we were not fighters.

When Taft was a student at the University of Southern California, he tried out for the Trojan band. He was a good trumpet player and passed the try-outs. Then he received a telegram saying that the band was all Caucasian, and he was not acceptable. He was president of the Chinese Students' Club, and he was urged by the members to take the matter up with the university president, Dr. Rufus von Kleinsmid. Together with Ed Lee (who later married Holly) and George Chan, who had also been rejected by the band, Taft went to see Dr. von Kleinsmid, but the president was adamant. The band was only for Caucasians.

Tom Leung family at the Pico home as Mr. Leung plans to send his boys to China. Seated: Mr. and Mrs. Leung. Standing behind: Lillie (left) and Mamie. In front from left: Taft, Monroe, Holly, Howard, William. On Mr. Leung's lap: Mincie.

"What if you had a Chinese band? You wouldn't want Caucasians in it, would you?" was his argument. Racial prejudice also ended Taft's hope of becoming a professional musician. He was barred from admission to the musician's union, despite the influence of his teacher, Samuel Porter, who was director of the pit orchestra at the Orpheum Theater and of the Los Angeles Police Department band. Porter recommended Taft to the orchestra leader of the Ocean Park pier dance hall (ironically, the same dance hall where I had been barred). But since he was not allowed union membership because of race, he could not get the Ocean Park job. "I guess I was born too soon," Taft says today.

At USC, the Chinese students formed a sort of clique. In order to avoid rejection, we never attended school social events and dances. We had our own activities and parties. I wrote for the *Trojan* and *Wampus*, the campus newspaper and humor magazine, and went to a couple of their social events, but I felt uncomfortable. By that time, my best friends were Chinese-Americans like myself. We had so much in common. Eleanor Chan was my best friend, and her sister Betty was Lillie's. They were more Americanized than we. Eleanor's full name was Eleanor Ransom Chan, which I thought sounded most elegant. She said I must also have a middle name; we finally, after much argument, settled on "Louise." After I went to work, one of my city editors dropped the "Mamie," and my byline read "Louise Leung." However, I was always "Mamie" to my family and friends of the early days, and still am.

CHAPTER 23

Food as Ritual

Anything new and novel interested Papa. He took Taft, William, and Monroe to the first sound movie in Los Angeles at the Tower Theater downtown. "It was a showing of such subjects as a wagon going over a bumpy road, chickens cackling, a man's whip smarting," Monroe wrote. "We all thought it was marvelous."

When the Graf Zeppelin came to town, it was on display at Mines Field, and, of course, Papa had to see it. Monroe was with him and wrote that when Papa got out of the car he was so anxious to get close to the zeppelin that he walked into a wire and bumped his head against it, resulting in a bruise over his right eye. His preoccupation showed up later in an amusing incident related by Monroe. The family was at dinner in Chinatown at some sort of celebration, and Papa got drunk. He was talking loudly and boisterously when he suddenly jerked his head to one side and stopped talking. Asked what was the matter, he said, "I thought I saw a zeppelin whiz by and nearly hit me!" That was one of the few times Monroe said he had ever seen Papa drunk.

Papa joined the nation in hero worship of Charles Lindbergh after his solo flight across the Atlantic. He went to the big welcome given Lindbergh in Los Angeles and talked enthusiastically to us about the flyer's feat. He held him up to us as a role model.

When club aluminum pots and pans were put on the market, the company introduced them by having demonstrators cook a free meal in your home. (Of course, you were expected to buy a set of the pots afterwards.) This intrigued Papa. A Chinese representative came to our home and cooked an American meal. The feature of these pans was that you could fry food without using grease. We all sat around our big dining room table, eagerly awaiting the meal, which turned out to be delicious. The demonstrator was a good cook as well as a good salesman. Papa was so impressed that he bought $80 worth, which was a lot of money in those days. "I know now that we were gypped," Monroe wrote. "I think my Dad was more attracted by the free meal than by the pots." But we got our money's worth because we used them for as long as I can recall.

One summer, Papa was visited often by Tom She Bin, the herbalist who was held in low esteem by the Chinese community because he had more than one wife. I had wondered why Papa had so much to discuss with him. It was only in recent years when I read about Kang Yu-wei that I learned that Tom She Bin was a follower of Kang and active in the local Empire Reform Society. His name was mentioned in some of the books about Kang, as was Papa's. Tom She Bin was a large man with a walrus mustache who always wore a wide-brimmed, black felt hat. He came to our house in a car driven by his eldest daughter, Ora. She was a couple of years older than Lillie. We were somewhat awed by her air of sophistication and worldliness. She taught us how to crochet, and we spent pleasant afternoons on our front porch, crocheting and gossiping; Ora liked to boast of her conquests. That was the same summer that Lillie and I had a crush on the pleasant, young, blonde soda fountain clerk at Carroll's drug store. We consumed at least two sodas a day in order to see and talk with Sam; fortunately he made us a small soda for which we paid only five cents. Ora went with us to see this paragon. She boldly invited him to go on a short ride with us on his break. To our amazement and delight, he accepted, and we went to the little park at Alvarado Terrace where we chatted awhile and took snapshots. Lillie and I wanted to pose with him but lacked the nerve. That was how the three of us passed the time while our fathers discussed Kang and the Reform Society. We lost Sam to a dazzling, blonde beauty named Mary who lived in the Doria Apartments adjoining the drugstore. Whenever she came in and took her customary stool at the end of the counter, Sam cut off his bantering with us and held long, intimate conversations with Mary. I hated that girl; I thought she spent far too much time at Carroll's.

Food was almost a ritual in our household. Papa loved rich food. He always had for dinner one or more dishes of chicken, duck, squab, or a big stuffed fish, together with several side dishes. On very cold nights, our parents enjoyed *da bin low*. This meant cooking food at the table on a grill that was operated by gas at that time. All the meat and vegetables were cut in small slices; each person would select his own food and hold it with chopsticks in a large vessel of boiling water on the grill. Abalone was a favorite food at these meals. Soon, the water would develop a good flavor from all the meats, fish and vegetables. Instead of rice, we ended the meal with a big mess of noodles cooked in the now delicious soup. *Da bin low* meant a lot of work — everything had to be cut up small to cook fast, but it was especially satisfying on a cold night. Another favorite dish of Papa's was *Yir sang* (raw fish). The filleted fish was cut in small spices to camouflage the fishy taste. Papa added chrysanthemum petals too. For those of us who couldn't bring ourselves to eat raw fish, there was a big kettle of *jook*. We put some of the fish mixture in a big bowl and ladled the hot *jook* over it. The heat was enough to cook the tender slices of fish. Sometimes, we had pork meat balls or chicken cooked in rice gruel. *Jook* was served for lunch or for *sui yea* (night-time snack). When Gee Sook was with us, he cooked rice in a big wok on the end of the wood stove. A crust of toasted rice formed on the bottom and sides of the wok. It was called *fan jui,* and we loved to eat it with butter or with tea poured over it.

On Sundays, we sometimes had dinner in Chinatown, usually at the Grand View restaurant. (This was, of course, in the Old Chinatown.) I hated to eat there because the places were dirty; I especially disliked the spittoons in the booths and the black chopsticks that always seemed to be sticky and dirty. We had spittoons at home, too, in the office and in the upstairs and downstairs parlors. I shuddered at them, too.

A big, juicy, tenderloin steak was Papa's favorite American dish. Once he brought some home for us to cook. We fried them on the stove, but he said they weren't properly cooked. A few days later, he brought home some more and said he would cook them himself. He wouldn't use the gas stove but had us fire up the wood stove and grilled them on top of it. The steaks were tender and juicy, and he was very proud of his culinary skill. It was the one and only time we saw Papa cook.

Lillie and I had our own eating program. When Mabel Johnson was with us, we started the habit of four o'clock tea, except that we had coffee, not tea. We had crackers and cookies with our coffee. Every night, Lillie and I had *sui yea*, consisting of rich pastry, cake or pie with something to drink. We indulged in this snack just before bedtime. Somehow, we didn't gain weight or get sick on this fattening, unhealthful regime. In addition, of course, we made frequent trips to Wallace's corner grocery for penny candy, and to Carroll's drug store for sodas. Our parents did not supervise our diet. Lillie bought our pastries at Young's Market, which had a reputation for fine foods. Even Mama liked their moon cakes; Lillie always brought home a box of the crescent-shaped, iced confections whenever she went there. They also carried tins of English cookies, which were another favorite of Mama's. When Young's Market closed, it was a gastronomical blow to our family. Beatty, our cook, introduced us to waffles. Waffles on Sunday morning became a custom. There were no electric waffle irons then. We used a big iron one that smoked up the whole kitchen. Our food bills were huge. Papa didn't like to eat the same thing twice in succession, so we didn't save leftovers. Visitors who dined with us were amazed at the amount of food thrown away. We were also profligate in the use of utilities. Papa liked plenty of light, and usually the whole three floors of the house were ablaze with lights. I never heard of turning off lights in a room when you left it, until I was no longer at "1619." We had no idea of the value of money because we weren't given allowances. We just asked for what we wanted, and it was usually given to us. When I got my first job and was offered $20 a week, I thought that was a large salary. I continued to live at home and let my pay checks accumulate until my purse was stuffed with them; then I'd deposit them in the bank. I didn't offer to pay anything for my support, and I wasn't expected to contribute. That was the Chinese way, so long as Papa was prosperous.

CHAPTER 24

Our Peerless Car

One of the childhood duties Lillie and I had was to *jung gwat* (pound bones) for our parents. We doubled our fists and pounded on their bodies wherever they wanted us to do it. Mama suffered from rheumatism, and she said the pounding relieved it. Much of the time, Papa liked it, to relieve tension and to relax. It was like a massage. We didn't like to do it because it was tiresome and monotonous. My parents knew how to get the most work out of me. They praised me and said how well I did it, so I did it as long as possible in order to outdo Lillie. When I'd slow down, they'd say, "Do it just 100 more times." I'd count each pound of my fists and then go on 100 more times just to win more praise. Sometimes, Lillie and I would *jung gwat* together for Papa. He closed his eyes, and when he seemed to be asleep, we would sneak out only to be called back. Occasionally, we'd get a nickel for our efforts. As the boys grew older, they had to take over this irksome task, much to the relief of Lillie and me. I didn't know if any of my Chinese-American friends had to *jung gwat*, though Mama said it was a common practice in China. During Papa's last illness, Mama stayed up many a night doing this for him when we were all asleep. When Mama had a headache, she would pinch herself on the bridge of the nose until it was red. She said it helped — something else she had learned in China.

Mama used a Chinese shampoo called *cha jay* to wash her hair, as well as Lillie's and mine. *Cha jay* was a dried grass or herb and and came in thin round discs, like a big phonograph record, and was purchased in Chinatown. Mama boiled it in a kettle of water on the gas burner in the second-floor bathroom where the babies' milk was warmed. When the water had steeped for some time, it was poured into the big bathroom sink where Mama washed our hair. *Cha jay* had a good, herbal Chinesey smell and made our hair silky, clean and shiny. Mama thought it was the only thing to use on Chinese hair; she wouldn't think of using soap. Our hair was washed only about once a month, until Lillie and I started having our hair marcelled. The marcel wave was the precursor of the permanent wave. It was done with a hot electric curling iron, and the resulting waves were stiff and deeply grooved; I'm sure it was very hard on our hair. We patronized a beauty parlor in the City of Paris department store, where we had our first American shampoos.

Sometimes on a summer evening, Papa would like to ride on the "P" car to the end of the line and take some of us with him. Los Angeles High School was at the end of the line, and Papa walked around the grounds to breathe what he called "good air." There were no houses there then, only open fields around the school. It was completely dark and quiet, except for crickets in the tall weeds. It made me feel lonely and homesick. Papa enjoyed the wide open spaces and he would stay a long time before we got on the streetcar for the ride home. Although Papa liked the country, we were all "city kids." None of us ever went camping — we couldn't imagine how that could be fun. Papa, too, liked comfort; he liked to stay in nice hotels and eat in a well-appointed dining room. Our family was distinctly not the type to "rough it."

Lillie graduated from Los Angeles High when she was 16 and then entered USC. About that time, Papa started talking about buying a car but said there was no one who could drive. Lillie and

I were so eager to have a car that we both offered to learn. (At that time, there were few restrictions on driving.) Papa bought a Peerless, which was considered a fine car, although I had been hoping for a Cadillac or a Packard. He paid $5000 cash — a high price then. Papa didn't believe in buying on the installment plan; he said people could get in trouble buying things they couldn't pay for. Papa hired a driving teacher, and Lillie quickly learned to drive. This was surprising because she did not seem to have any mechanical aptitude. I went along on the driving lessons, but somehow I couldn't learn. The Peerless was a large car that accommodated seven passengers. In addition to the roomy front and back seats, there were two extra seats. Even this was not enough for our big family. Papa had a board covered with leather made to place across the extra seats so it would accommodate four children instead of two. We had no garage and had to park about a block away. One morning, soon after she learned to drive, Lillie took the car out, and it stalled on the streetcar tracks. A street-car was coming, and it hit the Peerless, but Lillie wasn't hurt, and there was little damage to the car. In a court suit that followed, we won. The attorney said Lillie was a very good witness — she was cool and calm. She was a good driver, but she soon got tired of all the driving. She and I hated the Sunday rides because everyone stared at us so. Other cars would whiz by, hardly occupied, while ours was three rows deep. People would look and then stare; I got mad and stared back.

Papa's favorite place was Pacific Palisades Park. We carried a handsome, three-layer, lacquered lunch box full of fried chicken, potato salad, sandwiches, sweets, and tea. Getting started was a madhouse. Papa was always impatient to go; we children were mumbling and grouchy, trying to get things ready; Mama never cared about going, so when we finally got started, everyone was in a bad humor. There was always so much to lug — the lunch basket, blankets, and beach chairs (our parents wouldn't sit on the grass). Loaded down with all this, plus holding on to the younger children, we paraded across Ocean Avenue to the park. It was always crowded on Sundays, and we could rarely find an empty summerhouse. Usually, Papa took the boys for a walk after lunch. Once he brought a mah jongg set. We didn't want to play — we got stared at enough, without playing mah jongg in public. Papa never played it at home; he didn't like the game because in China it was associated with gamblers. He disapproved of all the mah jongg parties we had, even though the money we played for was put into a kitty for parties. One summer vacation, mah jongg was the rage with the Chinese USC students; they were at our house playing day and night.

A memorable day at the beach — it was very hot — was when we wore our bathing suits and went in the ocean (Mama and Lillie sat on the sand and watched). Papa had a very old-fashioned bathing suit. We tried to persuade him not to wear it, but it was the only one he had. None of us could swim — we just waded in the water. Papa sat in the water near the shore, letting the waves lap over him, oblivious of the stares and smiles of passersby. We children stayed as far away from him as we could. Papa enjoyed his dip in the ocean, but the next day he had a terrible case of sunburn. He moaned and groaned as Mama tried to ease his pain with salves and oils. He never went swimming again.

Another time, we took a trip to Big Bear Lake, planning to stay overnight. Lillie didn't drive this time. A Dr. Stevens, who lived in the neighborhood and took a liking to Taft, drove the Peerless. We packed a big lunch and started early in the morning. The road to Big Bear was called the Rim of the World, and it was rough, steep and mountainous. Our parents liked smooth, well-paved, wide roads so this ride was most unpleasant for them. We were all scared to death when Dr. Stevens met another car on a especially narrow part; our wheels were right on the edge of the road. Mama was all for going right back home, but there was no turning back. To make matters worse, it was hot, and Holly got car sick. Monroe was getting over the whooping cough, so the two of them were vomiting, and everyone was cross. When we finally got to the lake, it was a great disappointment. We had expected a cool, blue lake surrounded by greenery and flowers. Instead, the place was hot and dusty, and the lodge was not the kind of hotel we wanted. Papa didn't like it at all, and Mama was so exhausted she hardly cared. We knew we didn't want to stay overnight. After eating our lunch and resting in the lodge a while, we started down. Mama was too tired to make the long ride home so we stayed overnight in a hotel in San Bernardino. We started back after breakfast the next day. It was wonderful to be home again. It seemed that home was the best place for our family.

With Lillie in college, "1619" was becoming a center of activity for the young Chinese community. We began giving dances. They were informal affairs at first, with the phonograph providing the music. Later we persuaded Papa — through Mama — to allow us to hire a dance band, three pieces for $7 each. The dances were always given on Saturday night. All that day Lillie and I were in a frenzy of activity, rushing downtown to get our hair marcelled, preparing the punch, sandwiches, and cookies. Before dinner we rolled up the rugs and moved the furniture in the parlor and dining room. We opened the French doors between the parlor and the front porch and moved the dining table to the porch, where the punch was served. After dinner, it took us hours to bathe, dress, and put on our makeup. Although the band arrived at eight o'clock, the guests were hardly ever there, and we were on tenterhooks until they arrived. The band was hired to play until midnight; but we usually begged Papa to allow them to play until 1 a.m., although he had to pay overtime. There were many more men than girls, and some of the men were too shy to dance. Good men dancers were much in demand. Papa enjoyed these occasions, even when we increased the band to four players. A few times he embarrassed us by appearing in a tuxedo and dancing clumsily with some poor girl. A few of the students from China could play Chinese chess, Papa's favorite game, and he would ask one of them to come into the breakfast room and play. The guy would have to play several games and pretend to enjoy it when he would much rather be dancing with the young people. Our little brothers annoyed Lillie and me by skidding across the waxed floor and making loud remarks about us and our guests. However, our dances were nearly always successful and well-attended. We took satisfaction in the long lines of our guests' cars parked on both sides of Pico street. With the live music and good refreshments, "1619" soon gained a reputation for having the best dances. Sometimes, our parents would invite their close friends, herbalist Y.H. Chung and his wife, to our parties. They would play Chinese dominoes in the breakfast room and enjoy refreshments of chicken *jook*. Dr. Chung had relatives who had a ranch, and our family went there occasionally, visits Papa especially enjoyed. (Only recently I learned that Chinese Historical Society of Southern California president, Angi Ma Wong, is the daughter-in-law of the former Lillian Chung, one of the Chungs' daughters.)

Our parents liked having our friends at the house and made them feel welcome. Our house became the "home away from home" for many a Chinese student. Almost every day, one or more students (mostly men) would drop in and, likely as not, be invited by Mama to stay for dinner. The Chinese Students Club at USC met at our house; there was always a "social hour" after the business meeting — dancing, mah jongg, and, of course, refreshments paid for by Papa. Lillie was president of the club for several terms; she was a leader, always efficient and well-organized.

PERSONALITIES

CHAPTER 25

E Sow

E Gow, E Bok Foo's second son, went to China to find a wife. We called her E Sow. The first time they came to our home, we were all impressed by her; she was nice-looking and well-poised. It was soon apparent that she was the dominant one in their marriage; E Gow was mild-mannered and quiet. For example, she learned to drive a car, something E Gow never did learn to do. Papa, who did not drive either, admired her gumption. She and Mama became the closest of friends and confided in each other. They both loved to read Chinese novels and newspapers, smoke, and drink tea. E Gow and E Sow had four children, George, Edith, Herbert, and Baldwin. E Sow was a strict disciplinarian. Her children were not allowed to call us by our American names, as everyone else did, but by our kinship names; Edith still calls me E Goo Jeh (second cousin). When Baldwin was just an infant, E Gow was stricken ill and died. On the night he died, Papa and Mama were called to their home near the downtown area. When they returned, they looked extremely sad. I felt badly, too, because E Gow was my favorite relative; he had always been so kind and gentle. E Sow and the children moved next door to "1619" so they could be near our family and especially near Mama. Those were very difficult times for E Sow. She didn't get along with her father-in-law, E Bok Foo, who now, according to Chinese custom, was responsible for caring for his dead son's family. He refused to do so. They had many unpleasant quarrels, which she would report to Mama. Strong-minded and independent, she got a sewing job in a sweat-shop factory, and worked very hard to support her young children. They, especially Edith, assumed responsibility early. She did the washing and once got her arm caught in the wringer of the machine. Almost every evening, E Sow came to talk to Mama, who was a mainstay of support.

Things changed for the better when Kit King Louis came to Los Angeles; she needed a place to live and, somehow, she and E Sow got together. Kit King was a student from China; she had been attending Stanford, but came to Los Angeles because she decided to study sociology, and USC had the best courses. Not long after Kit King went to live with E Sow, a man came to the door. Kit King opened it and saw with amazement that the man looked exactly like pictures she had seen of E Gow. The man said nothing, but looked at her for what seemed a long time before turning and walking away. E Sow believed that E Gow had come to see Kit King for himself to make sure she would be good for his family. Apparently, he was satisfied. I had thought Kit King was the source of this story, but when I asked her about it later she said it was the first time she had heard of it. Perhaps it was a figment of E Sow's imagination. Kit King taught Chinese to help earn her way through school. Among her students were E Sow's children, along with Monroe and Mincie. Mincie says she was the best Chinese language teacher he ever had; today, he can read and speak better than any of the boys. Another one of Kit King's students was the famous detective story writer, Earl Stanley Gardner, who had a great interest in China. He and his wife used to drive Kit King to their home in Ventura each weekend, where she would give him lessons. When Kit King returned to China in 1931, the Gardners went with her and stayed for a while in her family's home in Canton. She worked hard at her studies, not participating much in the social life of the other students. She is now one of the foremost women in China, known by her Mandarin name of Lei Jieqiong. She holds prestigious positions, such as vice-chairman of the Standing Committee of the National People's Congress. She is a renowned sociologist who was instrumental in reviving the study of sociology in universities after its demise in 1952. She is still a professor at Beijing University and is famed throughout the country. She is extremely busy lecturing and traveling, but always has time to meet her old friends from Los Angeles. My daughter Jane and I have had many happy times with her and are always impressed with her energy and enthusiasm.

E Bok Foo's third son, whom we called Sahm Gow, had an herb business in Oakland. He was a tall, gregarious, good-natured man. His wife, Sahm Sow, was American-born. She spoke English without an accent and was a society-type matron. Their only child, Dorothy, was, in our opinion, completely spoiled, and the center of their attention; perhaps we were somewhat envious. Their life style was almost entirely American. On our infrequent trips to San Francisco, we always visited Sahm Gow and his family; they entertained us in their home and in San Francisco Chinatown. I enjoyed these visits because they didn't disapprove of our not speaking Chinese as most of our other relatives did. Ng Gow, E Bok Foo's fifth son, was a traditional Chinese and, as I learned later, a member of Kang Yu-wei's Reform Society. His wife, a portly, good-hearted woman, spoke the *say yup* dialect which I couldn't understand at all. They had a large family of seven or eight children. Ng Gow was also in the herb business. Say Gow, the fourth son, was a handsome bachelor who had a crush on Lillie, but nothing came of that because they were cousins. He later returned to China. Papa didn't seem to be close to any of these relatives. He sent money to his older brother in China, Bok Foo. According to Mama, this brother never thanked Papa for the money, just scolded him for not sending more. Bok Foo was Yum Go's father. Papa sent quite a bit of money to relatives in China; Mama complained that they kept importuning him for more. She was especially bitter when Papa was sick and had little income, but still the letters demanding money continued.

The only relative we knew from Mama's side was her nephew, Bui Hing Go. He came to this country in 1921 and attended USC. Papa paid his tuition and he lived at "1619." He was a funny little fellow who walked with his feet turned out like Charlie Chaplin, and was fanatically movie-crazy. One of the first things he did was to go to see Mary Pickford. He claimed he saw her, but we were skeptical. He also went to the college dances at USC, which none of us ever did. We couldn't believe his boldness when he announced he was going to the biggest formal dance of the year. He not only went, but was driven home afterwards by one of the most popular girls in school.

One day Bui Hing Go received a letter from China, telling him of the death of his father. Lillie and I were preparing refreshments for a dance that night; we heard him crying loudly, uncontrollably. We had never heard a man cry before. It was terrible. We didn't know what to do. Should we cancel the dance? We felt so sorry for him. His crying could be heard all over the house from his room on the third floor and would certainly put a damper on the festivities. We finally decided it would be impossible to contact everyone; we just hoped he would have more control of himself by evening. We went ahead, but not with our usual enthusiasm. To our amazement, he came to the dance with Rita, the pretty office girl who was working for Papa then. Bui Hing Go had a crush on her. He loved to dance — though he did it badly, and he enjoyed the party as though he had never received the letter.

Once he had to have a tooth pulled; he dreaded it as though it were a major operation. Afterwards, Mama had to administer to him like a child, going up to his third floor room several times a day. He was useless around the house. We were annoyed because he didn't even take his dishes into the kitchen as everyone else did. But he was a good student and spoke English fluently. He liked American girls like Rita and was also one of the many admirers of Faith Yang, who came to USC from Shanghai with her two brothers. Faith wasn't pretty, but was petite and charming. Our parents called her "Yang Kwei Fei" after the famous Chinese concubine because of the many students who flocked around her. Bui Hing Go got nowhere with her, nor with any of the girls he pursued. He believed in ghosts and told ghost stories that frightened us. Mama said there were ghosts in an old country like China, but not here. Papa didn't believe there were ghosts anywhere. Bui Hing Go went East to study and then returned to China, where he obtained a government position. Despite his idiosyncrasies, he was likeable, open, and honest.

Another relative who came to live with us and attend USC was Chuck Ga Sook's son, T.T. Taam. "T.T.," as we called him, was a strange and moody person. His relationship with his father was distant; I never saw them converse together. "T.T." had graduated from Canton Christian College and wanted to become a minister; Chuck was completely opposed to this. At times, "T.T." was jolly and good company; at others, silent and morose. Later, he went to San Francisco, became a minister, married and had a family. When he visited us years later, his personality had changed. He was self-confident, almost boastful, as well as self-righteous and pious. "Everyone in San Francisco knows me," he said.

CHAPTER 26

Papa Goes to China

It was in 1921 that Papa made his momentous trip to China. He wanted to explore for himself the educational opportunities for the boys as well as the political situation. He also wanted to make money by buying Chinese merchandise to sell in this country. We all went to San Pedro with him on the day in January that he sailed. He shook hands with each of us as we clustered around him. There was no kissing or embracing, even though he was to be gone for a year. Our parents were not demonstrative; we would have been surprised to see them kiss. We were brought up in the same way. They hadn't kissed us even when we were babies or young children; yet we all grew up with a sense of security and love of family.

Lillie and I told Papa we wanted him to buy us some silk stockings and silk underwear. Silk stockings were hard to get in this country at that time, and we knew that beautiful, hand-embroidered underwear was available in China. For some reason, Taft asked for toothbrushes and towels. Chuck Ga Sook was in charge of the office during Papa's absence, and the business went steadily down. Chuck not only lacked Papa's suave way of dealing with the patients, but Mama was convinced that he embezzled money from the accounts. Papa wrote home frequently asking that money be sent to him to buy more merchandise. Mama kept none of his letters, but we have many that she and Chuck wrote Papa. He even saved the ones Mama pressured us to write him in Chinese. (Perhaps Papa was more sentimental.) These letters have been translated and reveal that Mama had a much better business sense than Papa. He wrote that he was buying a large number of Chinese carpets to send home; she cautioned that they might be difficult to sell (she was proven right), and she also gave him advice on duties and tariffs. She suggested that he buy textiles, such as silk materials, that would appeal to the American public. Papa spent about $30,000 during his trip, Mama said. Besides buying merchandise, he gave money to relatives and friends. Only his elder brother, Bok Foo, and two sisters were still living in the old Tom homestead in Sun Duck county. A highlight of his trip was his visit in Shanghai with his revered teacher, Kang Yu-wei. Kang was old and poor, and Papa gave him money. Kang died six years later. Papa kept the letters and poems Kang wrote him during their long friendship. Since they are of historical importance, I have donated them to UCLA's Oriental Library. There is a resurgence of interest in China and in Kang and his writings; the documents can be of use as original source materials for scholars studying that period in Chinese history. I am sure Papa would be pleased that his letters from his honored teacher are being preserved instead of lying unread in family trunks.

The most unexpected thing Papa did on his China trip was to acquire a concubine (*gip see* in Chinese). This happened in Shanghai. The woman was much younger than Papa, and, from her pictures, she was not pretty. According to a letter Chuck wrote Papa, Mama had heard a rumor somehow that Papa had a woman, and she was furious. Papa had written for more money, and Chuck told him that Mama refused to send him any more. We soon discovered what had happened because Mama and E Sow had long talks about it every evening. Lillie and I were more amused than shocked. We thought it was strange that a man as old as Papa (he was 46 at the time) would want a second wife, but we felt sorry for Mama, who was obviously upset. Mama gave Papa an ultimatum: he could not bring the concubine to the United States and he would have to send money home to our family. In other words, he had to choose between the concubine (we called her the "gypsy") and Mama and the family. Mama said she didn't care if he stayed in China so long as he sent us money, but I'm sure she did care. She really loved Papa, and I'm sure he loved her, though he always had an eye for a young, pretty woman. I don't think he ever intended to bring the "gypsy" home to Los Angeles, or to stay with her in China; she was just a diversion for him there.

One afternoon in October, I was surprised to get home from school and find Papa had returned. He had planned to stay in China a year. He and Mama had a long talk in the second-floor living room, with the door closed, and after that, things went on as usual. We were most interested in what he had brought home for us. He did bring the silk stockings Lillie and I had requested, but we were greatly disappointed in them. They were heavy black and white seamless, dozens of pairs. American silk stockings had seams then, were like cobweb, and were beige in color. We didn't know what to do with all those stockings; we never wore them because no one wore white or black stockings. The only silk underwear he bought were two embroidered pongee slips. I wore mine till it wore out. We hadn't asked for jewelry, but he bought each of us three girls a long string of jade beads which are now quite valuable; I keep mine in a safe deposit box. I also received a jade ring cut in an unusual rectangular shape and set in gold, and a heart-shaped gold pendant, with a Chinese inscription on a gold chain. Taft got his towels, thick white ones, some as large as a blanket.

Papa's strangest purchase was a batch of small brown suitcases, rather cheap-looking. He thought he could sell them, though none of us could see why. We finally gave them away. Despite Mama's advice, he purchased a large assortment of Oriental rugs of all sizes. They were beautiful and expensive and a problem to store. They had to be kept clean and dry pending sale. Papa had a platform built in the basement, and the rugs were stacked on it. There was also a collection of art objects: porcelain vases, jade trees, cloisonne, and bronze buddhas. These were displayed in a large glass case on the second-floor hall. Papa tried without success to sell the rugs and art pieces to downtown department stores; perhaps he should have had an experienced salesman handle the deal. It must have been a couple of years — and after much frustration — before he sold everything to F. Suie On, who had the best and most modern store in Los Angeles Chinatown. Meantime, we used some of the rugs in our house. Papa said we might as well enjoy them. Even the younger children had Oriental rugs in their bedrooms. F. Suie On was a shrewd bargainer, and Papa lost a lot of money on the deal. Mama was quite annoyed. She said Papa was a poor shopper and should have heeded her advice to buy silk yardage, silk underwear, and jewelry. Even though she sat at home, hampered by her bound feet, she was actually more worldly-wise than Papa. Among the personal things Papa brought home were some photographs of the "gypsy." Naturally, he never mentioned her to us. We children joked about her (not in front of him) and eventually, Mama joined us in laughing about the incident. She did not object to Papa sending the "gypsy" money, but he stopped even this when he learned the "gypsy" was running around with men.

Papa did accomplish one of his goals. He visited the schools and was dissatisfied with them. The boys should finish college before going to China, he decided. Peking was his favorite city. He was disappointed in Canton, his native city, and gave up plans to build a house there. Nor did he like Hong Kong, where, he said, the Chinese were "bullied" by the British. He told us nothing about the political situation or about his visit with his relatives in the old homestead. His letters home, which weren't kept, would have given a good picture of the China of 1921. None of us were interested enough to ask questions. The communication barrier was part of the problem, and we felt no curiosity. I was relieved that my brothers had received another "reprieve" and would not have to go to China.

父親大人膝下敬稟者自別
尊顏時深系念比維
玉體康強
起居曼福為頌現屆春假
學習漢文兼學串句譯文及國語屢蒙
表哥殷勤指導頗覺進步
大姊欲購之淡藍洋緞女亦需用但要白色
方合用也家中各人平安乞毋
錦注耑此敬請
崇安
次女羅蘭謹稟 十年三月廿二日 美國羅埠郵寄

Author's letter to her father, Tom Leung, in China.
Courtesy UCLA Oriental Library.

William's Diary

William's diaries for the years 1922, 1923, and 1924 tell what life was like at "1619" from his viewpoint. He was 11 years old when he started his diary in 1922; Papa gave it to him, and probably one to Taft and to Howard as well. William wrote faithfully every night before he went to bed, telling exactly what he had done. Since he never dwelt on personal feelings, it is no invasion of privacy to reveal what he wrote. His days were full. "Us three kids" — meaning himself, Taft and Howard — were then going to Chinese school in Chinatown every day after American school, and on Saturday mornings. In addition, William took clarinet lessons, played in the school orchestra, and spent his spare time on his great love, gardening. He was the only one in the family who shared Papa's enthusiasm for planting. Of course, Papa never did any of the work; he didn't dirty his hands in the soil, but he knew just which flowers and bushes he wanted. From the time he started school, William was the one who did the planting, at Papa's direction. Sometimes he was given a nickel or dime for his work — he also did gardening for E Sow. He wrote of buying his own seeds, flowers and Chinese vegetables, including *yern say* (Chinese parsley) and *gwa* (Chinese squash). Under his green thumb, everything thrived. A typical day of his life, September 16, 1922, was chronicled like this:

> In the morning I went with Papa to buy some baby plants to put in the front. We went to the Japanese nursery. When we came home I planted them. After I got done planting I changed the body of my wagon. Then I watched the men fix the roofing paper on the roof garden. After that I rode my wagon. At 7:30 us three kids went to the Sunbeam Theater to see "Tarzan."

Another entry read:

> Today we went to the beach (Palisades Park). When we found a place to sit we rested for five or ten minutes and then ate our lunch. Mama gave us each 10 cents to buy some cotton candy. We went up the park again and played on the cannon for a while. After that Papa told us to walk with him. We went to the pier to see them catch fish.

William always recorded what he got on his report cards — his grades were fair — and told of making a taboret and a "half-lap" in a subject called "sloyd." He gave the titles of all the books he read and told of his attempts to put out a paper, first called the *Star* and then the *Dragon*. "Us three kids" made wagons and scooters together, played baseball, football and basketball in a nearby vacant lot and went to the movies at least once a week. When the blue wagon he had built and worked on over a long period was stolen, William expressed no anger. He gave the facts and nothing else.

Some other excerpts:

> We studied our Chinese lesson. I cleaned the fountain because Monroe and Mincie through butterflies in the water and made a fish bulge out his eyes. It cost 25 cents

for that fish. There was an accident near our house. No one was killed.

Tomorrow is Lillie's birthday so I bought her a 25 cents house plant. It looks beautiful. The six kids bought Lillie an 80 cents box of candy.

Papa, Taft, Howard and I went to the China Cafe to eat. We went home and then we four went to see "The Covered Wagon." Papa didn't like it. After supper we four and Monroe went to Tally's to see Harold Lloyd in "Girl Shy." Papa was pleased this time.

Today I went downtown shopping with Taft and Howard. We bought four 25 cents towels, 2 for Lillie and 2 for Mamie, and 75 cents (3) handkerchiefs for Mama. Then we went to Poly to play football. There was a Christmas party here tonight, USC students.

Christmas. We got up at 5:30 a.m, to see the presents. We got an indoor baseball from Paul to us three big guys, volley ball from Ed Lee to us three big guys, box of cookies from E Sow. I got stationery from Bob and Wes, football game from E Sow to three big kids, two boxes of candy, football, pants (football) and helmet.

On William's birthday he received two dollars, which he immediately spent on a Boston fern, his favorite plant. He was very careful in choosing it, even counting the leaves.

On Christmas, 1923, Papa gave him a small printing press. This led to an orgy of printing cards, invitations and stationery. "Us three kids" started taking orders from their friends who wanted printing done. Papa, Taft, and William made many trips to the American Type Founders to buy different styles of type. Since the boys were actually starting a little business, Papa bought a $100 hand press. "Our press came in the afternoon," William wrote. "All together, with leads, slugs, brass rule, etc., it cost about $150. Hildreth, our American friend, helped put things in order and helped Taft lock up the form. We printed a few blotters; it prints fine." The press was kept in the basement. Taft was the chief printer, assisted by William and Howard. The inventory increased, and they were able to print in color, with many different types of print faces. They made halftone pictures from Papa's herb books, and printed fancy invitations for our parties. Papa bought 5000 envelopes and paper for printing as business stationery. The press more than paid for itself. After the boys grew up, it sat unused in the basement.

The diary recorded the move of the herb business from 711 S. Main Street, where Papa enjoyed his most prosperous years, to the new Arcade building in 1924. The move was necessary because the landlord sold the Main Street building. The new office was on the mezzanine floor of the Arcade (on Broadway near Sixth). Lillie and I thought it was a fine location because there was a Leighton's cafeteria on the first floor. On our frequent shopping trips, we stopped there for lunch and dropped by the office to rest. We had our first taste of scones at Leighton's and tried in vain to duplicate them at home. Papa soon discovered that the new location was not good for business. There was no street traffic as there had been at Main Street. Only his previous patients continued to come to the Arcade, and Papa spent a lot of time just walking around the balcony. Business was so bad that by the end of the year, Papa moved again to his last office at 326 W. Ninth Street, just a few blocks from our first home at 903 S. Olive.

Papa had a narrow escape in the summer of 1924 when he fell off the streetcar at Pico and Union. According to William's diary, Papa had gone to the post office to pick up some jade. He was getting off the streetcar at our usual stop but was only on the second step when the car started up again. He fell under the car. Men ran to pick him up. Miraculously, he escaped injury but was sore all over. We were all frightened; it was what we called *nga yern* — an experience that makes you weak all over. This may be a Leung expression because I have never heard it used by anyone else. The boys had to *jung gwat* Papa to ease his soreness. Mama didn't want Papa to ride streetcars after that. She feared he was too clumsy getting on and off.

Papa had his hair cut at a barber shop on Pico near Union. One day he came home and discovered, to his horror, that his precious tie pin — a cluster of three large pearls — was missing. He didn't know if he'd lost it on the street going to or from the shop, or in the shop. The boys were immediately dispatched to retrace his steps. He feared it might have been crushed by street-cars or automobiles, but he was lucky. The valuable pin was found on the floor near the barber chair where he had sat. It could easily have been stepped on and ruined.

Taft learned to drive about this time, relieving Lillie of the burden of doing all the family chauffeuring. She had to drive the boys to and from Chinese school in Chinatown and take Papa's dinner to him at the office. Taft made short drives at first, going to E. Sow's house, picking up the children from school, and visiting his friends who lived nearby. Papa wouldn't ride with me at the wheel. I stopped too suddenly, drove too fast, and didn't shift gears properly. On one of our Sunday drives to Exposition Park, Lillie tried to give me a driving lesson. I don't know what I did wrong, but to Papa's disgust we had to be towed home. William told with pride how he was occasionally allowed to take the wheel of "our Peerless" and drive for a few blocks. He and Taft became car buffs and went to all the car shows. They became devotees of Fords.

William had a knack for coining words, He made up the word "do-vee," meaning "wonderful," "swell," "great," etc. For a while "do-vee" was used regularly, not only by our family and friends here, but even by our college friends at Berkeley and Stanford. It didn't last long, however. Not so with "monka," which William abbreviated from the Cantonese expression *mung jung*, meaning cross or irritable. "Monka" has become an established part of the Leung vocabulary. Even more rooted in our familial language is "ish," which William abbreviated from "ish-i-gug-gug," meaning repulsive. There is no exact English definition of "ish-i-gug-gug," actually, and I have never heard it used by anyone outside our family. William's word "ish" has a multitude of meanings, all negative. You are "ish" if you are bored, tired, unhappy, depressed, lonely. It has an all-encompassing expressiveness that makes it indispensable. The Leungs couldn't get along without it; our friends and their friends have adopted it. I have heard it used by the most unlikely people, who I didn't dream knew "our" word. Our parents never used these coined words — just the children.

CHAPTER 28

Lillie's Marriage

The big family event of 1924 was the engagement of Lillie and Peter Soo Hoo. William mentioned it in his entry of March 8, although the most important thing that happened that day for him was the purchase of two cans of lilies for 10 cents each, which he noted first. Then he added: "Pete and Lillie is engaged so there was an engagement party (eating)." The next day he wrote, after listing his day's activities: "Peter is going away to Portland, Oregon to earn money to support Lillie. He gave us each 50 cents (us kids)."

The engagement had not been easily achieved. Lillie had always been popular with the men and had had many suitors. Peter's chief rival was a rosy-cheeked young man named Peter Hsu who attended the University of Redlands and was the scion of a wealthy family in China. He had followed Chinese custom and asked Papa's permission to marry Lillie even before he asked her. This, of course, appealed to Papa, and he wanted Lillie to marry him not only because of his background but because he would take Lillie back to China with him. (I don't know how

Papa thought he could get along without Lillie; he had depended on her in many ways since she was a child.) Papa was dead set against Lillie marrying Peter Soo Hoo because he lacked Hsu's Chinese cultural assets. Lillie and Pete had been "going together" for some time and saw each other every day at USC where both were students. Romantic love didn't count much with Papa, despite his liking for the American life style, but Mama said she would never force her girls to marry against their will. (She probably recalled her own desperate unhappiness at her arranged marriage even though it turned out well.) It was undoubtedly her influence that finally persuaded Papa to consent to Lillie's engagement to Pete. Until then, there was quite a bit of tension, with Hsu at our house almost daily. Lillie was nice to him and allowed him to escort her when a crowd of us went to the beach or for a drive. After Hsu lost out, he returned to China. Months later, he sent me a beautiful Chinese doll; that was the last we heard of him.

Papa resigned himself to Lillie's engagement to Pete. Pete came from a big family; they had a store on Apablasa street in old Chinatown where they also lived. His mother had died before we knew Pete, and his father was blind. Pete and Lillie had a big church wedding with a full entourage of attendants. Their honeymoon was spent in New York where Pete was delegate to a Shriners' convention. Lillie said she was homesick the whole time. Their first home was a tiny apartment in a court not far from "1619." They invited us, the immediate family, to lunch one day soon after their marriage. The small living room was crowded with tables and chairs to seat us all. Lillie made a delicious lunch, but as soon as we had eaten, Papa said it was time to go. On the way home, he said their place was too small. He needed plenty of space, big houses, big rooms. Later, Pete and Lillie rented a house on Burlington Avenue within walking distance of "1619." Actually, Lillie spent more time there than she did at her own home. Her life went on much as it had before her marriage. She continued to do the family shopping. By this time, we no longer had a cook. Beatty had left for some reason, and the black cook who followed her, named Ridgeway, was by no means the gourmet in the kitchen that Beatty was. Ridgeway left because she said the tile floor in the kitchen was too hard on her feet. Also, our parents were tired of American cooking. Although Mama had never learned how to cook in China, she somehow picked up the basics and gradually could turn out dishes that pleased even Papa. Lillie learned from her, and together they planned and cooked the family dinners.

Pete got a job as an engineer with the Department of Water and Power and soon became a leader in the Chinese community. He was active in many organizations and was one of the first Chinese to become a Shriner. He was also an excellent artist and designed some of the Christmas cards Papa sent to patients. Later on, he became the spark plug in establishing the new and present Chinatown. Papa never regretted his acceptance of the marriage. Busy as she was, Lillie got a job in the Chinese consulate. As usual, she made herself indispensable and worked herself up from clerk to the consul. She greatly increased her knowledge of Chinese. Besides all this, Pete and Lillie had two children, Peter Jr. and Patricia (Patty), who spent most of their time at "1619."

HARD TIMES

CHAPTER 29

Papa as a Tong Member

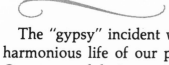

The "gypsy" incident was the most serious rift in the mostly harmonious life of our parents, but there were other quarrels. One occurred during a trip to San Francisco in our new red Stutz, of which we were all very proud. Papa, Mama, Taft, William, Howard, and I were on this trip, with Taft driving. Outside Santa Maria, he was stopped by a cop for speeding. Papa and Mama were very upset and bawled Taft out in Chinese. Perhaps this intimidated the cop, but we persuaded him not to give us a ticket since we were only a little over the speed limit. The incident put our parents in a bad mood, and, by the time we got to San Luis Obispo to spend the night, everyone was cross and tired. Mama wanted to rest and have a smoke in the hotel before going out to dinner, but Papa wanted to eat immediately. Mama said he was trying to rush her when there was no need to hurry; Papa accused her of "chasing" him home when we were barely started on our trip. They were angry at each other all the way to San Francisco, where Papa took the train home. The rest of us stayed on for about a week, but it wasn't much fun without Papa. Mama didn't enjoy it and was exhausted. When we got home, Papa was in a good mood. He had found Holly ill with a bad rash on her feet, and had given her herbs to clear it up.

Another incident we all remember was when Papa was beginning to lose his health and was irritable on occasion. Mama was preparing to cook a squab one day but discovered there were none of the herbs she needed. This made her cross, and she said to Papa, "How can you run a business when you don't have the herbs?" Papa retorted angrily, "If you can run the business so much better, why don't you run it?" He had always given her money every day for household expenses, but after the quarrel, he gave her none. When Mama sent the boys to the office for money he would say, "She has plenty." It got so we were having plain rice, bread, and peanut butter for our meals. When Papa came home at night, he went up to the library and arranged his books, paying no attention to Mama's scoldings. This went on for about a week; then he finally gave her $100, and all was well.

Mama was always more practical than Papa on money matters, and this led to disputes. He spent money unstintingly. It took a lot of money to support a family of ten, and he always wanted the best for all of us. He was often dunned for money by his older brother and other relatives in China, and he generously sent money to them regularly. Mama approved of this, although she often complained that the more he sent, the more they demanded. Mama's relatives wanted him to invest in their projects. One had a rubber plantation in Singapore and wrote Papa long letters asking him to invest in it. He wanted to invest, but Mama was against it and wrote her relative that Papa didn't have the money.

Although Papa was excellent at promoting his own business, he had no business sense. His worst mistake was getting involved in a fishery company at the behest of two of his good friends, Mr. Chan and Mr. Lew. He invested $10,000, against Mama's advice. Then, at the urging of his friends, he loaned another $5,000 by taking out a mortgage on our home at 1619 W. Pico. The friends promised that they would repay the $5,000 themselves if the fishery failed. So, without getting their written promise to repay, Papa went to the bank with them, took out the mortgage and gave them the $5,000 check. Only then did he ask for something in writing, but Chan and Lew said, "That's not necessary between friends." Mama was livid. She had been strongly opposed all along to the initial investment and especially to the mortgage on our home. The fishery failed; Chan and Lew refused to repay the $5,000. Papa took the case to court, but lost when he was unable to produce the endorsed check. Chuck Ga Sook had thrown it out with some other checks "because he was pocketing so much of our money himself," Mama said angrily. "If Papa had been able to produce the check, he would have won. It was enough to make you vomit blood." We had never seen Mama so incensed. Her eyes flashed, and her voice rose when she upbraided Papa about this. The mortgage was indeed a serious matter; it was to dog us for years as we tried to scrape up enough money to pay the interest and avoid losing the house.

In his desperation, Papa made what Mama considered another bad mistake. He took the advice of his friend, Tom She Bin, that he should join a *tong* to retrieve his money. *Tongs* in Chinatown were notorious in those days. They were secret societies that had started out as guilds where men banded together to protect their interests, but they evolved into gangs. Periodically in Los Angeles Chinatown there were wars between rival *tongs*, with violence and killings. We were horrified when we learned Papa had joined a *tong*; we felt ashamed because we had always regarded *tong* members as no better than gangsters. Mama said, "Papa was not the kind of person to be a *tong* member." He had placed himself in extreme danger. A *tong* war broke out, and Papa, as one of the most prominent members of the Bing Kong Tong, was a prime target. Lillie had to drive him to the office and back every day because it was too risky for him to ride the streetcar. It was a time of great tension and worry, not knowing from one day to the next what might happen. The *tong* could do nothing to get the $5,000 back, so Papa finally ended his membership, to our great relief. We had to pay off the mortgage as well as about $2,000 interest. Mama was understandably bitter about this whole episode. Papa learned, too, because he made no more such investments. It proved again that, despite her insulation from the real world because of her bound feet, Mama had an astonishing amount of good judgment and sound common sense.

CHAPTER 30

Papa's Death

I graduated from USC in 1926 with no idea what I was going to do. While trying to decide what kind of job I could get, I took some articles I had written in journalism class to several newspaper offices, hoping to sell one or more. To my amazement and delight, the *Los Angeles Record* not only bought an article about the month-old banquet celebration for my nephew, Peter Soo Hoo Jr., but offered me a job at $20 a week. Being a reporter had not occurred to me; I did not think a Chinese, and especially a woman (women reporters were rare in those days), had the remotest chance. *The Record* was the smallest and feistiest of the six dailies in Los Angeles, and the editors were willing to launch me as the first Chinese reporter on a metropolitan daily in the country. It proved to be a gratifying career. After the *Record*, I worked at various times on the *San Francisco News*, *Chicago Times*, *Los Angeles Daily News*, and *Santa Monica Evening Outlook*. Being Chinese, I learned, was not a liability in my job. Among the good assignments I received were the covering of the gala visit here of Madame Chiang Kai-shek during World War II, the trial of Al Capone, and the interviewing of celebrities such as Albert Einstein and Mortimer Adler, and countless movie stars.

Local Los Angeles journalists and photographers covering District Attorney Asa Keyes' trial, 1927-1928. The author is second from right, first row.

Papa was sick for at least two years before he died in 1931. Before then, he had been exceptionally healthy. I don't recall his ever being sick or missing a day at the office. He was always overweight because he loved rich food. At first, he tried to doctor himself with herbs, but, when he failed to improve, he went to an American doctor. This physician diagnosed the illness as Bright's disease (kidney disease) and ordered Papa to cut down on rich food and wine. Papa developed a bad cough and lost weight. Mama cooked all kinds of Chinese dishes she thought would be healthful for him, such as *dong gwa* (melon), *yin wah* (bird's nest soup), and *gee mah woo* (almond paste pudding), but Papa insisted on fried foods and rich dishes. The illness made him irritable. He went to the office every day, even though many nights he slept little because of his cough. The boys, getting up at night, saw Mama in her green bathrobe sitting on his bed to *jung gwat* him. She did this for hours to relax him. There were times when he seemed better, and we were encouraged, but then he would relapse. He got so thin his suits sagged on him, and he had them altered. Even during his illness, he was careful about his appearance and wanted his suits to fit just right.

Business was slow because it was the beginning of the Depression and this worried Papa, too. Sometimes he felt too tired to work a full day and came home early. He was sensitive about his illness and was angered if it was mentioned. At that time, we were buying our fruit and vegetables from a Chinese man who came by every day with his wagon laden with fresh produce. He had been doing this for years and had become a good friend. We called him the *gwa-choy* (melon-vegetable) man, and all the children would run out to see what "goodies" he had. Often, he gave us samples of fruit. Mama and Lillie discussed what we needed, and the *gwa-choy* man brought in our purchases, always stopping for a chat with Mama. We used to tease her that he stayed so long because he liked her. He did chores for us, such as killing chickens. At first his wagon was drawn by a horse, but later, he got a Ford truck. Our long and happy association with the *gwa-choy* man ended one day when Papa came home early from the office because of his illness. In his document, Monroe gave a graphic description of this incident:

> We knew him so well and he knew us, that this Chinese vegetable vendor was welcome at any time, anywhere. It so happened that this man saw my dad. He said, *"Gum jo fan lay?,"* meaning "Home so early?" We all expected my dad, who had just come home from his office, and was standing by the dining room door smoking, or preparing to smoke his water pipe, to reply "Yes." But instead he said in Chinese, "What business is it of yours? What do you care if I come home or not? We don't want any of your old vegetables. Get out." This made us speechless, at first. We couldn't believe that our dad was saying such a thing to an old friend of the family, who had been selling vegetables to us for years. This man was speechless, too. He just looked terribly hurt and walked quietly out with his head bowed

down. We were hurt, too. We felt awfully sorry for him. Ma told Mincie to run out and buy something from him and tell him that Dad really hadn't meant what he said. Our dad was in very low spirits to bawl out a family friend like this. He never at any time lost his temper in front of anyone outside his family. I don't remember any time. After the vegetable man left, my Ma, after sending Mincie out to buy something, turned to Pa and said quietly, "Why did you say that?" But he didn't reply, merely walked out on the porch. No one else dared to say anything because Pop would certainly bawl them out, too. Ma only asked that question once; she knew that Dad was sick and tired and might scold her too . . . I'll always remember exactly how I felt when Pa said the first few words. I was afraid to look up because I didn't want to believe it. In fact I thought it was a dream . . . Dad's voice was, or it seemed to me at the time, to be strangely soft and at the same time it sounded like he was sorry he was saying it, but kept right on because he had started it.

It is evident what a strong impression this incident made on Monroe, who had great affection for the *gwa-choy* man. "I'll always remember his wagon and horse," he wrote, making a sketch of it. "It was a very high wagon with a roof on it. The horse was quite good. When he started to go, the wagon rattled and the scales on the wagon would swing from right to left. The old top rod and the supporting iron posts would swing in the opposite direction." Once the horse fell down, or got hit by a car, and had to be lifted up from the street so that it could continue. Sometimes Monroe got a ride with the *gwa-choy* man on the way home from school. But after the incident with Papa, we never saw him again. We had to buy our fruit and vegetables from the grocery store.

Monroe also described other incidents of Papa's illness:

When Dad began to cough, my Ma made him stop eating greasy foods. My mother made the man at the office who was cooking all his night meals stop cooking such foods that were bad for his cough. His cough would stop for awhile, then begin all over again. We immediately began to accuse the man — Kwong Sook — at the office for serving greasy food. Kwong Sook would insist that Pa made him cook such-and-such food. Once, about a year before he died, he had a coughing spell in the living room which continued until his face turned from red to purple and black! He was merely sitting on the davenport when he had this attack. Peter, me, Lillie, William and Taft saw it. I was sitting at the table reading when I noticed his coughing was unusually long, looked up and saw that something was wrong. Peter said, "Get a glass of water!" I ran into the kitchen where I saw Ma; I told Ma what the water was for; she didn't seem to believe me at first. (I was always kidding — all my life.) But I nevertheless got the water, ran out and there I saw Pete massaging Pa's back. Pa was a dark purple by this time and I nervously tried to shove the water into his mouth. His cough by this time had become weak little sounds, finally no sound at all, just jerking of his head and abdomen. But he came through OK. This experience will always haunt me. I thought about it in school all the next day. The first words he said when he came to were, "What are you trying to do? Why all the fuss? I thought someone was trying to hit me or hurt me." Something like that was what he said (in Chinese, of course). After that, whenever I heard him cough I thought another attack would come; it was an awful feeling of suspense. That's why I was glad I didn't go to the show with him on Sundays. He took Mincie because I was getting too tall; I'd have to pay adult's admission price. Of course as he was getting sick, he wouldn't go to as many shows as he used to. He had another attack before this I think. I believe William and Holly saw that one.

I was working in Chicago during the worst of Papa's last

illness, but from Monroe's poignant descriptions I can picture the events leading to his death and the family anguish on the day he died:

Poor Ma used to sit up with Dad and massage him all night. Ma didn't ask us kids because we had to go to school. I used to get up about 1 or 2 a.m. to piss and I would see Ma sitting at the foot of Dad's bed massaging his legs. The room was dark but I could see Ma's green bathrobe. I used to tell Ma to go to bed and I'd continue for her. I did this only once or twice. I wish I did it more now. Most of the time we wouldn't even know Ma was sitting up. . .

I remember on the day Dad died, the doctor had just finished injecting something in his arm and told him not to get up. This was about 9:15 a.m. But Dad got up when the doctor left. He got up and Ma was holding out his bathrobe so that he could extend his arm into the armhole. He just toppled over. Ma couldn't lift him so she ran out to the hallway to call Howard and Taft who were sleeping upstairs on the third floor. William (home for the summer from UC Berkeley) had gone to the drug store to get some physic medicine. Howard and Taft lifted Pa up on the bed. Called the doctor. I was awakened by Ma calling loudly for Howard and Taft. It was like a dream. Something told me an awful thing had just happened, but I refused to believe. I heard lots of commotion, then Holly or someone came in and told me Dad had fainted or something like that, so I got up. I walked past Dad's room and looked in to see him lying on the bed with his head at the foot of the bed and his feet where the pillows were — no I'm mistaken. He was lying diagonally across the bed with his feet dangling over the foot of the bed. Right at that moment I knew he had died. Taft, William and Howard were massaging his legs and back. I went up to the third floor and washed my teeth and face. Came down. By that time the doctor had come. He looked into Dad's eyes, felt his heart and then without a word walked over to Ma who was sitting in her little red leather chair in the parlor, grasped her hand and walked away. We knew that was the official announcement of Dad's death. The doc went downstairs to call up. Lillie was in the room with Ma too. She had called Peter at work. Holly called other relatives. The next day which was Sunday was terribly sorrowful. Our relatives decided on the funeral, which was to be on Saturday. It seemed terribly long for us. We wanted it to be earlier, but naturally had nothing to say. When Mrs. Tom How Wing (E Sow) saw the doctor leave his car without closing the door and dash in our house, she sensed that something was wrong and came over. When she came over, she cried loudly, and made me feel terrible.

The day was June 6, 1931.

I received a telegram from Peter saying, "Papa died this morning. Please come home immediately." I was in the newsroom of the *Chicago Times* when the wire was brought to me. It was a terrible shock. I had never realized how serious his illness was. I don't think anyone in the family did. Papa was only 57. We all thought if Papa followed his diet he would get well. He had worked right up to the day before he died. We all regretted we had not insisted he get a second opinion; we knew nothing about his doctor.

I took the first train home. All during that long journey my grief was compounded by my realization that I hardly knew Papa. I had never had a real conversation with him. It was a sad homecoming. Mama wept that it was hard to get along without Papa; they had been together for so long. When I went to the funeral home to see Papa, I was shocked at how thin he had gotten; he didn't resemble the Papa I last saw. The relatives took the initiative in arranging a big funeral. Following Chinese custom, the cortege passed Papa's office and our home on the way to the cemetery. Mama didn't go to the funeral; we feared it would be too great an ordeal for her. She was worn out from the long months of sitting up with Papa at night and the shock of his sudden death. We also followed the custom of giving a wrapped coin and piece of candy to each person at the funeral as he or she left the cemetery. The coin was to be spent immediately. The candy was to be eaten to leave a sweet taste after the grief of the funeral.

CHAPTER 31

Hard Times

Without Papa, our authority figure and head of the family, our home was like a ship without a rudder. Financially, we were a disaster. Papa had no life insurance because he didn't believe in it. (He once got a letter from an insurance company describing their policies and was so angry he had me write them never to send him their literature; I tried to explain that this was just advertising, but he was adamant. He didn't want to be reminded of death.) Because of the fishery investment debacle, there was the mortgage on the house which had to be paid off. There was very little money in the bank. Relatives wanted to take over Papa's business, saying they would pay Mama a certain amount, but Mama didn't trust them; she didn't want to be at their mercy. She showed her mettle then and her independence. With Papa gone, she was the head of the house, and she refused to allow the relatives to coerce her in any way, but she did not antagonize them. She had always remained in the background as a good Chinese wife but now she proved that she was going to hold the family together by sheer determination, despite her inexperience.

She was pressured even from China. Papa's older brother, Bok Foo, wrote urging her to bring the family back to China, saying that was where she and her children belonged. All the time she had lived in this country, Mama had longed to return to her homeland, but when Papa died, that dream died. She was practical. She realized that we would find it difficult to adjust to life in China. We had been brought up as Americans and could speak little Chinese. How would we make a living? She herself had experienced too much independence to want to live with her husband's relatives. She wrote a polite letter to Bok Foo saying she and her children must remain in America. He never wrote again, much to Mama's relief.

Taft, William, and Howard had to quit college. Taft had just completed his junior year and Howard his first year at USC. William had finished his first year at UC Berkeley, the university he had set his heart on since childhood. Taft was 22, and Mama decided he was old enough to take over the herb business with the help of Kwong, the druggist, who was paid a wage besides room and board at the office. Probably Mama would have gone to the office herself if she'd been able to speak English. Taft was the front man who met the patients and talked with them. The prescriptions were the same as Papa had prescribed for different ailments. Not surprisingly, this arrangement did not work too well. Business had already fallen off because of the Depression and because Papa's illness had prevented him from working full time or performing well when he was on the job. With Papa's death, only patients who had been seeing him for a long time, sometimes for years, continued. New patients were few and far between. The mail order business from Canada continued to bring in some money.

There were times when Kwong could not be paid his $110 a month salary on schedule. He became impatient. Mama decided to close the office, get rid of Kwong, and run the business from home. She had learned how to *jup yerk* (fill the prescriptions), and Taft met with the patients. He relayed their complaints to Mama, who used Papa's prescriptions to treat them. Kwong opened his own herb business in Pomona; he had a list of the names and addresses of Papa's patients and made use of it. He told Mama that some patients had complained to him that they had got herbs that made them worse.

It was an extremely traumatic time for Mama. The family had suddenly been catapulted from prosperity to poverty. The few dollars the herbs brought in were not enough to support the family. The boys went job-hunting in a market where there were no jobs — it was the depths of the Depression — and where they had no qualifications. I sent what money I could, but it was little. William doggedly pounded the pavements and finally landed a job as a janitor at an old but prestigious apartment house on Wilshire Boulevard called the Gaylord. He worked long hours doing all kinds of menial duties; because he was so willing and uncomplaining, he became a valued employee. His wage was small, but it fed the family. There were no longer the duck, squab, and chicken that were daily fare when Papa was alive; sometimes there was just rice and *foo yer* (bean cake). We considered it a great stroke of good luck when William got Holly a job with a family in the apartment house. She was to look after the small children, do all the housework and laundry, and some cooking. The wage was $25. Holly was used to hard work, but this was extremely hard; she worked for 12 hours a day. She did the laundry in the basement and was afraid because there were rats down there; she had William stay with her. After a week's work, she was not paid the $25 and discovered that the wage was $25 a month, not a week. Hard up as we were, Mama had her quit the job. She was really angry that Holly had been exploited in this way. Besides, Holly was indispensable at home. (She had graduated from Los Angeles High school just a week after Papa died and was unable to attend the excercises.) She had always been put upon by her brothers but took it good-naturedly. Now that she had finished school, she took on more and more of the household chores, and could hardly be spared for an outside job.

Monroe got an after-school job sweeping floors in a big chain store. One of our relatives happened to see him at work and complained that it was degrading to the Tom family to have a member doing such menial labor. Mama heard about this and was extremely bitter; the whole family was indignant. We deeply resented this interference by relatives. Monroe was doing honest work, and we needed every penny we could get.

The whole family — in their spare time — took part in a project at home, sorting walnut meats from shells, to make a few dollars. Lillie wrote me about this in a letter dated November 5, 1931. "We have been so busy sorting walnuts that I have not had time to write. We are so slow at it that we can only finish 100 lbs. in one week — others do that much in a day. They pay six cents a pound, but there are about 20 to 30 pounds of shells in each bag so it is hardly worth wasting your eyesight on it at the rate we are going." Apparently, the family picked up speed doing this tedious job because in a letter a month later Mincie, who was then 14, said: "We picked walnuts in about 3 1/2 days. Of course Mama doesn't help. We haven't received the money yet, but after the second bag we'll have the money. These walnuts are nice and big, so it is easier to pick than the first bag." How much was ever received from this tiresome, boring project was not recorded.

In the same letter, Mincie mentioned troubles with our uncle, Chuck Ga Sook, who had opened an herb office in San Luis Obispo. "He sent a telegram as follows: 'Jailed by medical board unable to pay fine borrow hundred dollars wire immediately.' Since we borrowed $200 from him for Papa's funeral he thinks he can get his money back this way. Mama knows he has at least $1000 in the bank. He thinks that he's not going to get his money back. That's the whole proposition. We haven't got the hundred dollars and he knows it. That's what we told him in the telegram. Needn't worry about this affair. Mama is taking it as a minor effect on her burden. She talks to E Sow and when the affair is mentioned she laughs usually."

The Depression was taking its toll. Mincie gave a graphic description of the situation in a letter dated December 22, 1931.

> Times are surely getting worse. People come to our house begging for clothes and work. Recently, a man about middle-aged, poorly dressed and seemed very hungry, rang our doorbell one Sunday morning, asking for some clothes. William answering the door and promising he would give some clothes. To his surprise, William gave the man a new suit hardly worn; this suit

was much too small for William. Rejoicing, contented and happy, he shook hands with William and bade him goodbye. A week later he came to our house again, this time with two policemen. Holly answered the door this time as William was at work. "Well," said the policeman, "This man is accused of stealing a suit; he says that your brother or husband (Ha ha) gave him this suit." "Why yes," says Holly. "I remember this man clearly coming to our house on Sunday morning and my brother giving him a suit." "What color was the suit?" Holly was questioned. "Blue," she said. "See," said the accused man. Holly asking why they came, the policeman said that he was jailed because of having a new suit. Well, from this incident you can see that a poor man can't have a suit without being jailed. I think things are getting worse than better.

Mincie went on to write about our financial situation: "I suppose you're anxious to know how much we got for 21 days. Not so good, not so good. Guess. $184.42. Needn't send any money though. The interest on our taxes and house is terrible, $80 every three months. Ugh! I approve the farm plan; that's the only hope or perhaps go back to China. William knows how to farm and that was Papa's plan that we should buy a farm and let William have the experience."

At times Papa had talked about taking the family back to China and buying a farm which William could manage. But the continuing political turmoil in China prevented any serious consideration of this plan. I was glad this was mostly talk because I didn't want to live in China.

William was now the mainstay of the family. He never complained about working so hard and so long at his janitorial duties. He gave every cent of his meager earnings to Mama. She gave him a few dollars now and then so he could buy seeds and plants for the garden. He spent all his days off in the yard, watering, planting and cleaning — it was what he enjoyed most of all.

Taft wrote me not long after the herb business was moved from the downtown office to "1619":

Since we moved the office back home, business has been pretty fair and I hope it keeps up. March was the first month we were here and we made the biggest sum so far this year. We even made more than when we were at the store and we took in more new patients. I think we just had a stroke of good luck that's all. I don't believe we can do as well this month, but you can never tell. Even if we only make $200, we can use every cent of it for ourselves and not have to put it back for rent and wages. Well, we put off our relatives for a while and shouldn't be bothered with them any more. They wanted to run the business and eventually control it but I think it is better even to go on as we are.

He made no mention of how he and Mama coped with the problems that must have arisen.

CHAPTER 32

Mama the Matriarch

During Papa's lifetime, the house was always spic and span; nothing was allowed to go unrepaired. Now, with the struggle to survive absorbing everyone's energy, the place deteriorated. There was no money for maintenance. Only the garden — because of William — looked unchanged. The house paint peeled; the furnishings were shabby and worn. Previously, we had eaten in the breakfast room at a table covered with a white linen cloth. Now, the family ate in the kitchen at a round table covered with white oilcloth. The sugar was kept in a tin instead of the silver sugar bowl of Papa's days. He would have shuddered at our change in life style. The breakfast room became Mama's sitting room. She reclined all day on a blue couch next to the French doors that overlooked the garden. Beside her was a low table where she kept her thermos of tea, cigarettes, ash tray, books and newspapers. On the other side of the table was her old, red leather chair, which was often occupied by E Sow. She came over every day to chat with Mama, and the two would sip tea, smoke, and read newspapers or novels when they were not commiserating with each other on their troubles. They had a close companionship, which was a boon to them both.

Mama's day started about 9 a.m. when she got up, washed, and smoked her water pipe, sitting on a stool in the bathroom. She combed her hair in the pompadour style she had adopted when she first came to America. For this task, she used the gold lacquer cabinet with the folding mirror that she had brought from China. Then she tucked a fresh handkerchief — she used men's large linen handkerchiefs — in the opening of her long gown, sprinkled some Florida water (she liked it better than perfume) on her hands, and was ready to go downstairs for the day. She wore high bed slippers (it was difficult to find a size small enough for her bound feet) and walked down the steps carefully, holding on with one hand to the banister.

She made herself some oatmeal for breakfast, eating it without milk. She boiled a kettle of water for her thermos of tea, which was always kept filled. After eating she had another smoke on her water pipe before going into the breakfast room to recline on the couch and read the Chinese newspaper, which arrived daily from San Francisco. There was nearly always someone at home with her. People came and went, because "1619" was still a hub of activity. Mama welcomed her children's friends; they felt at home there, and Mama was at the heart of it all, a tiny, indomitable matriarch. Visitors always went first to the breakfast room to chat with Mama, even though communication was sometimes difficult. Lillie got home from work about 3 p.m., and she and Mama would plan what to cook for the evening meal. Mama went to bed about 10 p.m.; one of the boys would help her up the stairs to her room, and she would have a final puff on her water pipe.

Gradually things improved. Howard got a job as a houseboy. William quit the apartment house job and went to work for Albert Quon, a schoolmate of Mincie's at USC who became successful in the export-import business. Although this job was not as menial and hard as the janitor's work, it was not at all fulfilling for William. He was poorly paid and worked long hours. He had tried without success to get enough gardening jobs to make a living.

The herb business finally petered out. It was more and more difficult to get herbs from China. Taft, who had taken accounting at USC, got some jobs keeping books and doing income tax for Chinatown merchants. His dream of becoming a professional musician was stymied because Chinese were not admitted to the musician's union. However, he soon established himself as an accountant and was able to work at home.

Another project to make money was to sell Chinese tea from door to door. Mincie early demonstrated his ability; he was the best tea salesman in the family. Later, after his graduation from Los Angeles High School, he worked his way through UCLA doing a variety of jobs, such as janitor in a drug store, movie "extra" in such films as "The Good Earth," and a stint as proof reader for the state legislature in Sacramento. But his best money-making project was a gimmick he originated that earned him about $50 a week, a large amount in those days. He sold chopsticks in Chinatown — which many people were doing, but his novelty was to write each customer's name on the chopsticks in Chinese. He had been a good student of Chinese, and knew enough to write American names in Chinese using phonetics; what he didn't know he made up, and no one was the wiser. His booth in Chinatown was always surrounded by customers, but inevitably, his idea was stolen by others and his profits decreased. Not only was he able to pay his way through UCLA (tuition was only $27 a semester then), but he also helped with family expenses. William also tried to sell novelties in Chinatown. He had attractive art objects such as cloisonne pill boxes, ceramic pillow vases, and miniature copper novelties, but he just wasn't cut out to be a salesman.

Howard quit his houseboy job to work at the National Dollar Store, which was operated by Chinese. He also got Holly a job there as cashier, but she had to quit when her hands broke out with a rash (caused by handling dirty money, Mama believed). Later, she worked as a cigarette girl at the Biltmore Hotel and in a dress shop. Howard went on to be a bartender in various Chinatown restaurants. He also had a job as a line inspector in a machine shop that manufactured aircraft parts.

Monroe wanted to go to art school, but there was no money

for that, so he did odd jobs. (Papa had recognized Monroe's talent for art and one Christmas, when Monroe was about 14, bought him a drawing board, which he hid at the office. Monroe happened to see it, but didn't let on.) Against the odds, he got a job as a beginning artist at Warner Brothers cartoon studio. Monroe had a wonderful sense of humor, demonstrated in the cartoons he drew. In later years, he occasionally sold cartoons to magazines.

Mama's financial worries diminished. Everyone turned over nearly all their earnings to her, and she handled the household expenses. The sorest times were definitely over. The prosperous, carefree days of Papa's time were gone forever, but so were the days when the family didn't know where the next meal was coming from.

The author/journalist with noted actress Anna May Wong.

GENERATIONS

CHAPTER 33

Marriages

My marriage to a fellow newspaper reporter, Arnold B. Larson, was a terrible shock to Mama. Interracial marriages were not commonplace as they are now, but she resigned herself to the *fait accompli.* In time, after we returned to Los Angeles, she grew fond of my blond, blue-eyed husband, and he always felt the greatest affection for her, even though our marriage eventually broke up. We had three children, Stan, Jane, and Dan.

February, 1937, was an important milestone in the Leung household. Holly and Ed (Lee) had become engaged the Christmas before and wanted to be married on Valentine's Day. Ed was the son of long-time family friends. Taft and Esther (Loo), whose family we also knew, had been "going steady" for a long time. Chinese custom decreed that older siblings should be married before younger ones and Mama thought it unseemly if Holly married before Taft, so Taft and Esther set their wedding date for February 4. They were married at "1619" in the downstairs parlor-dining room. William did a beautiful job of decorating, using flowers donated by a Japanese nursery across the street, which we had patronized for years. He turned one end of the room into a bower of greenery and blossoms. That was where the couple exchanged vows. Rows of folding chairs were set up, and the French doors leading to the front porch were opened for the overflow of wedding guests. It was a festive occasion. Taft and Esther took up residence on the third floor, where there were two bedrooms, bathroom, library and roof garden. The second bedroom later became a nursery for their two children, Larry and Geraldine.

Holly and Ed had a full-scale wedding at the old church near Olvera Street. Ed, who had just graduated from the USC dental school, was doing free dental work at the church clinic. There was a big wedding banquet afterwards. Ed's parents had to defray most of the expenses because Mama was in no position to do so. The newlyweds set up housekeeping in an apartment. Holly was sorely missed at home where she had done so much to keep the house going by cleaning, cooking, and washing. But she, like Lillie, was often at "1619." She and Ed had four children, Priscilla, Warren, Virginia and Cherylene. The latter two took ballet lessons at a young age, and for several years Holly was extremely busy as a "show biz" mother. The girls were successful working in films and TV and did a stint in Las Vegas; Holly chauffeured them from studio to studio as well as to their dancing lessons.

Mincie graduated from UCLA in 1939 with a degree in accounting. The next day, he boarded a Trailways bus to New York City to see the World's Fair. He liked New York so well that he decided to stay for a few months and got a job at the Fair, resorting to his old gimmick of writing people's names in Chinese. On his return trip by bus, World War II began. Back at home, Mincie tried his hand at selling insurance, bookkeeping at the Ninth Street market, and selling refrigerators to Chinese restaurants — "ish" jobs as he described them. His selling took him to San Francisco, where he decided to apply for a job at both IBM and Pan American Airways. He was delighted and amazed, a few days later back in Los Angeles, to receive a letter from IBM offering him a job as bookkeeper in the Honolulu branch. He learned afterwards that the offer was made over the strenuous objections of the branch manager, who didn't want an Oriental in his office. The salary was $150 a month, munificent in those days. Mincie was happy to be started on a "real" career, and Mama was overjoyed. Pan Am also offered him a job, a few weeks later. Mama and E Sow were among the group who saw him off on the Lurline to Honolulu. He did well with IBM and even got a night job teaching accounting at Honolulu Business College. He made an unbelievable $200 a month and sent Mama a lot of money.

The family expanded still further in 1941 when Howard and Rose Yee were married. Their wedding was solemnized at "1619," with William again doing a superlative job of decorating the front room. It was another memorable occasion. The newlyweds moved into Papa's bedroom. Howard and Rose had two children, Jeanette and Howard Jr. There were now many seated around the kitchen table for the evening meal when everyone ate together. Each of the working family members contributed what he could to the household funds, which Mama managed. It was a traditional Chinese arrangement.

Mrs. Leung and her sons who served in World War II.
Left to right: Lt. Lincoln Leung, U.S. Marines; Cpl. Monroe Leung, U.S. Army Air Force;
S/Sgt. William Leung, U.S. Army; T/Sgt. Howard Leung, U.S. Army Air Force.

CHAPTER 34

World War II

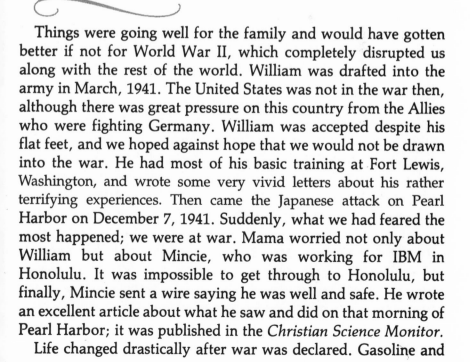

Things were going well for the family and would have gotten better if not for World War II, which completely disrupted us along with the rest of the world. William was drafted into the army in March, 1941. The United States was not in the war then, although there was great pressure on this country from the Allies who were fighting Germany. William was accepted despite his flat feet, and we hoped against hope that we would not be drawn into the war. He had most of his basic training at Fort Lewis, Washington, and wrote some very vivid letters about his rather terrifying experiences. Then came the Japanese attack on Pearl Harbor on December 7, 1941. Suddenly, what we had feared the most happened; we were at war. Mama worried not only about William but about Mincie, who was working for IBM in Honolulu. It was impossible to get through to Honolulu, but finally, Mincie sent a wire saying he was well and safe. He wrote an excellent article about what he saw and did on that morning of Pearl Harbor; it was published in the *Christian Science Monitor*.

Life changed drastically after war was declared. Gasoline and sugar were rationed; there was constant fear that the Japanese would attack the coast, and we were required to have blackout curtains to keep out the light. Periodically, the sirens would sound when an unidentified plane or vessel was sighted. Then, everyone was to clear the streets; motorists parked and turned off their lights. Everyone drew their blackout curtains. It was frightening. We Chinese had a special fear. We were concerned that we would be mistaken for Japanese, who were the objects of American suspicion and hatred. I had an experience that dramatically portrayed this phenomenon. My son Stan and I were living in Topanga then, and once a week we went to "1619" by bus and streetcar. On one such occasion on the bus, I was reading a letter I had just received from Arnold, who was working in San Francisco. He mentioned a Japanese American friend of ours who was in a concentration camp. I noticed that a man sitting next to me seemed to be trying to read my letter; this annoyed me, and I tried to hold the paper so he couldn't see it. After a while, he got off. When we got to the end of the bus line where we were to transfer to the "P" streetcar that took us to "1619," two policemen got on the bus. I was astounded when they came to me and told me to follow them off the bus. When I asked why, they simply ordered me to follow. It was humiliating. The bus passengers gaped and whispered as we were led off the bus. The policemen ordered us into a police car. Seated in the front was the man who had been sitting next to me on the bus. I knew immediately that he was the reason for our detention, but I couldn't understand why, except that he had been trying to read my letter. I saw red. I yelled at him. It was all I could do to keep from striking him with my purse, but I assaulted him verbally with vehemence. He said nothing, but one of the officers warned: "Be careful, lady. You can explain when you get to the station." This didn't deter me from berating him and the police all during the short ride. "I'm an American citizen. What right have you to stop me? This man was trying to read my letter." I could think of nothing in it that could lead to this drastic action. Stan was about eleven or twelve; he was embarrassed at my defiance. The man kept his silence.

I was taken to the captain's office at the station. He asked to see the letter I had been reading. At first I refused, saying it would violate my right to privacy, but when the captain threatened to arrest and jail me, I reluctantly turned over the letter. He read it from beginning to end. It was about things that should be done around the house, family matters, etc. Finally, the captain said, "What about this reference to the Japanese in the internment camp?" So that was it! I had read the letter so hurriedly that I'd forgotten about that. I explained that we had this Japanese friend who had recently been sent to a concentration camp, and my husband had learned she was doing well, despite the difficulties.

I told the captain I could prove I was Chinese. I had been born in Los Angeles, graduated from USC, worked on newspapers, and had a brother in the service. I added angrily that the man should be arrested for reading my letter and causing me and my son so much humiliation. "He was just doing his duty as a patriotic American citizen," the captain said. No doubt the man, who had been whisked out of sight in the station, envisioned himself as a hero, catching a Japanese spy bent on overthrowing the country! By this time it was late, and I knew my family at "1619" would be worried because we were long overdue. The captain offered to have his men drive us to "1619," but I didn't want the shame of riding in that police car again. I demanded that he give us carfare, which he did, probably only too happy to be rid of me. There was no apology, however, nor would he give me the name of the informer.

The incident showed how paranoid much of the American public had become. They couldn't tell Chinese and Japanese apart, so every Oriental was suspect in the eyes of fanatics like the man who alerted the police about me. I was so furious that I went to the *Los Angeles Daily News,* where I knew a popular columnist, Ted LeBerthon, a former colleague. He wrote an excellent column citing my experience in detail and pointing out the dangerous attitudes that were taking over in America. I took special pleasure in mailing two copies of the column to the police captain, requesting that he send one copy to the informer.

Although most of my family and Chinese friends were sorry for the Japanese Americans being herded off into camps and losing everything, we were not outraged at their treatment, nor did we feel that it was unjust and unconstitutional at the time. Primarily, we felt fortunate we were Chinese and not Japanese. Japan had been at war with China for years, and we were accustomed to thinking of Japan as the enemy. Mama and E Sow hated Japan with a passion as China's foremost enemy. Long after World War II ended, I had to be careful not to give E Sow a gift made in Japan.

William's experiences in being mistaken for a Japanese were not just infuriating, as mine was, but life-threatening. He told of almost being shot by Americans while he was overseas fighting the Japanese as an infantry machine gunner. Once, he was even taken prisoner for a short time until he could prove his identity. William was much calmer in his reaction than I, even though he had been in real peril.

Taft was the only son in our family who was not drafted. Each family with several sons was allowed to keep one at home; Taft was needed to carry on the remnants of the herb business. After William, Howard was drafted and went into the Army Air Corps. He was sent to North Africa and was stationed at the Marrakech airbase, where he worked as an instrument mechanic. He stayed there for 33 months. All that time, we had no idea where he was because servicemen were not permitted to tell their whereabouts. In his letters home he tried to give us hints about where he was, but they eluded us. He stayed on the airbase most of the time and saw no combat.

Monroe was lucky. He managed to delay getting drafted until November, 1942. "After weeks of excuses," he says, "including mentioning Mama's bound feet," he finally got his notice of 1A. He was sent to a camp in Sacramento, where he got a job as a drummer in the Army Air Force band. After two-and-one half years, he got an even better deal; he was transferred to the motion picture animation unit in Culver City, the old Hal Roach studio, because of his work at the Warner Brothers cartoon studio. He lived at home, just like a civilian; Ronald Reagan was also assigned to Culver City, as a captain, and lived at home too. Monroe used to see Jane Wyman, to whom Reagan was married at the time, pick him up every day at 5 p.m.

Mincie showed his usual know-how in dealing with the draft.

He got a full-time clerical job at the Pearl Harbor naval shipyard in order to obtain a draft deferment. He was able to handle his IBM job in a few hours every evening, which he did with his boss's permission. He even managed to teach a few classes at Honolulu Business College, so he had three jobs. But after two years, the draft board refused to renew his deferment and ordered him home to Los Angeles for induction. The board permitted him to go to New York for a few weeks. There he learned that the Marine Corps was looking for officers who knew some Chinese, so he went to Washington, D.C., for an oral interview. He was asked to translate an article in a Chinese newspaper. The officer in charge said he passed and would be commissioned a second lieutenant in the Marines, provided the draft board did not beat them to processing the papers. After a few days of anxious waiting at home, the papers arrived, and he was ordered to report for officers' training at Quantico, Virginia. "I was incredulous," Mincie says. "Me, a Marine! I still feel uneasy about it. Of course I was overjoyed and gloated over the draft board when I showed them the official appointment." The Chinese lessons Papa had insisted on had paid off for Mincie. He was trained as a combat intelligence officer and later was sent to UC Berkeley for an intensive course in conversational Mandarin. As an officer, he was paid $150 a month and $100 to support Mama; in addition, IBM paid him a quarter of his salary, so he had more money than ever to send Mama. Even after the war ended in August, 1945, the Marines continued his schooling. In December, 1945, he sailed for Tsingtao, China, with the 1st Marine Air Wing, where, he said, "I did absolutely nothing." He was the only one of us to see pre-Communist China and was able to compare it with the China he visited afterwards. He was not discharged from the Marines until June, 1946.

Mama courageously saw four of her five sons go off to war, one after another. She didn't shed a tear until her grandson, Peter Soo Hoo Jr., was drafted. Her eyes were red with weeping the morning he went overseas. She thought of him as a young boy and couldn't accept his being sent to fight in the war. Pete Jr. had just graduated from Polytechnic High School when he was drafted; after basic training, he was sent to Italy as a machine gunner. The war in Europe ended soon after, and he was sent back to this country to be re-deployed for a planned invasion of Japan. Fortunately, the war with Japan ended, but Pete Jr. was not discharged until April, 1946.

As it turned out, none of the boys saw combat except William, but he experienced enough to make up for all of them. He fought in at least six major battles from Attu to Okinawa as a machine gunner in the infantry, one of the most dangerous assignments in the army. He was the first in our family to be drafted, and the first to go overseas. Of course, he was unable to give even a clue as to his whereabouts. I found out his first field of battle by accident. At that time, I was working on the *Los Angeles Daily News*, and one day I was sent to interview a family whose son was fighting in the Aleutians. The newspapers were filled with stories of the battles of Attu and Kiska, where the soldiers battled the Japanese in freezing cold and blinding blizzards; these were the first confrontations with the Japanese in World War II. I was sick at heart when the family told me to which infantry division their son belonged — it was the same as William's, so I knew he was on Attu. We didn't tell Mama — no need to worry her. Finally, after the battle, we got a letter from William. Since he had no writing paper or envelope, he wrote on a carton from his rations, and fastened it with wire. Unfortunately, we kept none of his wartime letters, but I wrote an article about his letter from Attu:

> We thought desert maneuvers were rugged but they were child's play compared with this. We went without hot food for days and lay for hours in freezing water. You don't mind the cold when you see tracer bullets coming for you. We had to climb volcanic peaks when we were completely exhausted, fighting an unseen enemy in dense fog. After the battle, we had the gruesome task of burying the Japanese dead, many of them headless after their suicidal last charge in which they blasted themselves with grenades.

Somehow, he was able to send home some Japanese dishes he

had salvaged from the fighting. They were heavy white crockery marked with a blue star. "They were filled with food when I found them," he wrote. For years these dishes were displayed in the china cabinet in the downstairs parlor. There was a picture in the *Daily News* of Larry and Priscilla displaying the dishes "liberated" by their Uncle William. It is sad that these souvenirs were somehow lost in the final move from "1619." Attu was just the beginning of William's ordeal. He was promoted to sergeant and was awarded a Bronze Star "for heroic achievement." The citation, which was published in the *Daily News,* said, "While delivering supporting fire for a platoon of tanks, Sgt. Leung's machine gun squad was subjected to heavy enemy mortar fire. Ordering his gunner to take cover, Sgt. Leung immediately manned the machine gun and laid accurate and sustained fire on a group of the enemy armed with satchel charges." Fortunately, this award was not lost. Holly has it on display in her rumpus room. William took good care of his men, and they remained his devoted friends after the war. His death in 1968 brought many letters from them, attesting to the deep affection they felt for him. William didn't like to talk about his war experiences, and we didn't press him. We knew that his best friend had been killed, and William had the sad task of writing to the family and sending them his few belongings.

In those days, every ring of the phone and the doorbell was answered with dread. We didn't know what to expect. Death did strike, but in the most unexpected way. Peter, Lillie's husband, suffered a sudden stroke and died in the spring of 1945. It happened one night after we had a big family dinner for a longtime college friend, Wesley Thom, who was visiting from Canada. Pete was his usual genial self. He, Lillie, and Patty went home afterwards. While preparing for bed, Pete suddenly collapsed and lost consciousness. He was rushed to the hospital but died the next day. It was a painful shock for Lillie and for us all. I can recall Mama in the kitchen that morning, shaking her head in disbelief, her eyes red. Pete had always been so healthy and energetic. He had been working very hard, not only at his engineering job at the Department of Water and Power, but also in establishing New Chinatown. He and Lillie also had a gift shop on GinLing Way in the new project, so he worked day and night. Hundreds attended his funeral, which was well-publicized. Peter was recognized as the foremost leader of the Chinese community and was often referred to as the unofficial mayor of New Chinatown. His name is still mentioned whenever the history of Chinatown is recounted. Peter Jr., who was in the army in Italy, was not allowed to return home for his father's funeral. Lillie displayed the utmost courage throughout the ordeal. She must have been numbed by the shock. She continued on her job at the Chinese consulate; she and Patty stayed on at the Burlington street house, although they were at "1619" much of the time. Peter's death was especially tragic because he was only 44 and at the height of his career and community accomplishments.

CHAPTER 35

After the War

When the atom bombs fell on Hiroshima and Nagasaki, our reaction was great relief that the long war was ended. Everyone knew that the United States was girded up for an invasion of Japan. We wondered how much longer William could have survived. Howard and Pete Jr. would certainly have been sent to Japan, and perhaps Mincie and even Monroe. We didn't dwell on the horrors of unleashing the atom bomb or its potential for destroying the entire world; we were just happy that the long nightmare of the war was over. Words cannot express the joy at "1619" when all the boys were finally home, safe and sound. There were no kisses or embraces, but we celebrated with a big dinner for family and friends. Mama never looked so happy, with all her family around her. Today, I believe the bombing of Japan was wrong, but I am still thankful that my brothers were spared the horrors of an all-out invasion of Japan.

The household at "1619" settled down into routine after the war. The family expanded still further when Monroe married Rose Wong in 1946. We called her Rose Two to distinguish her from Howard's Rose, who was Rose One. In order that the newlyweds could have their quarters at "1619," Mama gave them her room and moved into the pink bedroom that was originally Lillie's and mine. The second-floor parlor was divided. Howard and Rose One and Monroe and Rose Two each used the half adjoining their bedrooms. Monroe and Rose had four children, — Kirby, Linda, Timothy, and Corinne. Thus "1619" became a traditional Chinese family compound. As the numbers increased, the round oil-clothed table and the adjoining rectangular table in the kitchen became more and more crowded at dinner time, the one meal when the whole family ate together. But there always seemed room enough to squeeze in one more chair. Mama was the matriarch who ruled the household. Each son contributed his share to Mama, and from this common pot, the household expenses were paid. There must have been bickerings and resentment from so much "togetherness," but I remember no open quarrels, which is remarkable. Mama liked having so much of her family under one roof — it was the Chinese way. It was so different from the American way in which parents expect their children to leave home after they have finished school and have jobs. American children, for their part, are eager for this independence. Only economic disaster causes them to seek refuge with their parents, and when this occurs, it is an unhappy situation for all. So the Chinese family compound at "1619" in the midst of metropolitan Los Angeles was an unusual phenomenon.

It seemed that every year Mama had red eggs and chicken to distribute for the increasing number of grandchildren. All the children, except Lillie's children and my son Stan, were close in age. Those who didn't live at "1619" came often to visit. All birthdays and holidays were celebrated there, and it was bedlam when the whole family gathered. Mama was, of course, a most indulgent grandmother. She always had a store of *lai see*, candy, and gifts to give the children. None of the children spoke Chinese, so they couldn't converse with her. All they could manage was to greet her respectfully as "Ah Po" and thank her for her gifts, but they grew up with great affection for their gentle grandmother.

Taft attained success as an accountant for several companies in the wholesale produce market. He obtained a state license as a public accountant, and his practice grew to the point where he had 16 or more clients at a time. His most prestigious position was with the highly successful men's clothing establishment of Boshard-Doughty at Sixth and Olive Streets. He set up the books for this firm and later was named secretary-treasurer of the corporation and a member of the board of directors. Taft was so modest about his accomplishments that it was not until I was collecting data for this history that he told me he is listed in *Who's Who in the West* and *Who's Who in America* 1976/1977. The citation states that inclusion is limited "to those individuals who have demonstrated outstanding achievement in their own field of endeavor and who have thereby contributed significantly to the betterment of contemporary society." He has also belonged to organizations such as the Los Angeles Produce Dealers Credit Association, the National Society of Public Accountants, and the California State Board of Public Accountants.

After the war, William wanted very much to start his own flower nursery, but feared he wasn't a good enough businessman to succeed. He finally decided against taking the risk and took a job at the post office, not as a mailman, but as a letter sorter in the office, a job he held for the rest of his life. Although it was far beneath his talents, it gave him security and enough money to buy the good things he liked, a nice car (which he always kept in top condition and immaculate), a fine stereo system, and finally, his own home. As soon as he earned enough money, he bought a Capehart, the state-of-the-art stereo of those days, and books and records. At the end of his eight-hour day, he could forget his job and listen to music and read. He loved to drive, and on his paid vacations he took long car trips, sometimes visiting his old war buddies. William never married. We all thought William was Mama's favorite child; he was so thoughtful of her, but he was that way with everyone. At Christmas, the children always opened Uncle William's gifts first. His gifts were not tinsel-wrapped and beribboned; they came in plain paper bags, but they were always something very special. He himself dressed plainly; he wore a suit only at weddings and funerals.

Howard wanted to go into business for himself after the war. He learned how to repair watches and operated a "Time" shop for seven or eight years. Then he bought a small grocery store on the south side of Los Angeles. Because of many robberies in the area, he sold the store after five years, and went back to tending bar in Chinatown, which he still does. It is a job which suits him well, and over the years, he has made many friends. Howard's hobby is cooking, and he has become a premier chef. His spareribs are especially outstanding. His contributions to family feasts are always gobbled up immediately. He and Rose love to go to Las Vegas, to the horse races, and to play mah jongg.

Monroe went back to work at Warner's cartoon studio after the war. However, he never liked animation, and after two years, he quit and went into commercial art. He worked for a number of firms and was quite successful. He put all his four children through college and also attained his dream of owning a Rolls Royce. He has great artistic talent, and we all treasure his drawing of "1619," which he made from a photograph and gave to us one Christmas. He also has a wonderful sense of humor. He still draws cartoons occasionally, and we call on him when we want art work done. His "letters to the editor" — usually on matters of racial prejudice, which truly irk him — appear occasionally in the Los Angeles newspapers, signed with his name but giving his address as Beverly Hills.

Mincie returned to his IBM job in Honolulu after his discharge from the Marines in 1946. IBM sent him to Endicott, New York, for training as a sales representative, and then sent him back to Honolulu. He was successful in his new and prestigious job, making his annual sales quota and winning trips to the mainland where he always, of course, visited Mama. After some years of this, he tired of the job. He quit IBM and invested in a Dairy Queen franchise in Honolulu. After a few months of working long hours with no money to show for it, he realized he had made a disastrous mistake. He gave up his ice cream stand and went to New York City. There he worked as a data processing manager for several corporations until 1964. By then, the "rat race" of the business world got to him, and he decided to go into teaching because of the easier schedule and long vacations. He got a job as assistant professor of accounting and information systems at Pace College in New York City. He also obtained his MBA degree in

The family in 1947.
Standing, left to right: Howard Leung, Lincoln Leung, Stanley Larson, Arnold Larson, Larry Leung (child), Taft Leung, William Leung, Monroe Leung. Seated, left to right: Mrs. Howard Leung with Jeanette, the author Louise Larson with Jane, Mrs. Tom Leung, Esther Leung with Geraldine, Mrs. Monroe Leung with Kirby.

management from New York University. Teaching was what he really enjoyed, he discovered. Like William, Mincie is a bachelor.

Pete Jr. worked for the Veterans Administration for a short time after the war and then enrolled at USC where he graduated with a degree in marketing advertising. He followed in his father's footsteps and took a job with the Department of Water and Power. He first worked in market research; he was then promoted to sales promotion planner, and then to conservation and association consultant. Another milestone was his marriage to Lucy Lee. Trudy and Karen, two of their four children, were born during Mama's lifetime, giving her the great joy of being a great-grandmother.

CHAPTER 36

End of an Era

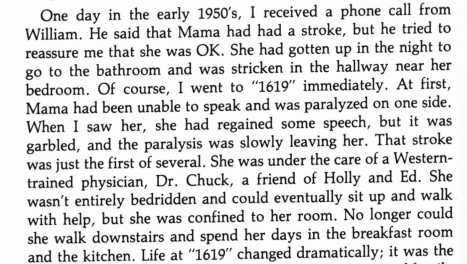

One day in the early 1950's, I received a phone call from William. He said that Mama had had a stroke, but he tried to reassure me that she was OK. She had gotten up in the night to go to the bathroom and was stricken in the hallway near her bedroom. Of course, I went to "1619" immediately. At first, Mama had been unable to speak and was paralyzed on one side. When I saw her, she had regained some speech, but it was garbled, and the paralysis was slowly leaving her. That stroke was just the first of several. She was under the care of a Western-trained physician, Dr. Chuck, a friend of Holly and Ed. She wasn't entirely bedridden and could eventually sit up and walk with help, but she was confined to her room. No longer could she walk downstairs and spend her days in the breakfast room and the kitchen. Life at "1619" changed dramatically; it was the beginning of the end of the old homestead as the center of family life.

By this time, Lillie had built a duplex in the Silver Lake area on a lot which Peter Sr. had purchased. The house was ideally designed to give privacy to two families. Lillie and Patty had their part of the house (Patty lived there until her marriage to Dick Lem); Pete Jr. and Lucy had the other half with plenty of room upstairs for their expanding family. The house was the scene of many happy family gatherings. Lillie was an excellent cook and enjoyed entertaining.

Holly and Ed had their first home on La Salle Street. Although Holly was extremely busy raising her four children, she came to "1619" every day to see Mama and to cook special treats for her.

William was the first son to move out of "1619" after Mincie. He used the money from the G.I. bill to buy a large lot on W. 124th Street near Broadway, and had a house built according to his own design — two bedrooms with a bath between, a large living room, and kitchen. He furnished it carefully and tastefully. The big backyard was an ugly expanse of dirt at the time. William did a prodigious amount of work transforming the yard into a fabulous park. This was his opportunity to apply his love of gardening creatively. He planted trees and shrubs, flower beds, and ground cover, selecting just the right kinds. In no time he had a lavish garden with meandering paths and even a dry creek. One year, he had a big strawberry patch and had enough berries to supply the whole family bountifully. William enjoyed his home enormously. It was always immaculate. He spent hours in his living room listening to music on his new stereo and enjoying his garden through the big glass doors.

Mama liked going to William's house. After her strokes, William wanted her to live with him. It would be easier for her to get around in a one-story house. Somewhat to the family's surprise, she made the momentous decision to move from "1619" and into William's house. We thought she would get homesick for the place Papa had built, where the family had lived for so long and happily. But strangely enough, once she moved, she never once mentioned "1619" again — never asked who was living there or whether it had been sold. William did everything to make her comfortable. He furnished her bedroom with the bed and dresser she had had at "1619." He bought a chaise lounge so she could recline in the front room where she could look through the glass doors into the garden. Everyday Lillie or Holly, sometimes both, visited her, always bringing a favorite Chinese dish which William could warm up for dinner. Then Taft bought a lot on 126th street, just across the alley from William's, and built a nice three-bedroom house. When Taft and Esther moved in with their youngsters, Larry and Geraldine, it was nicer than ever for Mama. On weekends I came with Jane and Dan so William could have some time to himself. Mama enjoyed sitting on her chaise and watching Geraldine and Jane dancing in Taft's living room, which had glass doors facing William's house. On holidays and birthdays, the whole family gathered at William's to celebrate instead of at "1619," which was gradually being abandoned. Howard and Rose and their daughter Jeannette (Howard Jr. was born later) moved to a home on Norton Avenue, near Rose's relatives, where they still live. Monroe and Rose were the last to leave. They and their children, Kirby, Linda, and Timmy (Corinne was born later), moved to the Crenshaw area where they lived for many years until they bought their present home in Monterey Park.

It was a wrenching experience to leave the home where we had so many happy times, a place that represented our childhood and youth. Walking away and leaving "1619" was like abandoning an old and dear friend. Selling "1619" was difficult. The neighborhood had deteriorated badly; it is now called the Pico-Union ghetto. We sold "1619" to a dentist who had his office and home there. His endeavors failed, and the place became a boarding house. Our old home looked like a tenement, a far cry from the brand new, freshly painted house in prime condition that we had moved into in 1913. It was occupied by several families. As we drove past we saw shabbily dressed children playing on the sidewalk, or an old man or woman sitting dejectedly on the front steps. One day, some years later, I received a note from an old newspaper friend, Ray Rowe, who had visited "1619" several times. He enclosed a picture from the *Los Angeles Times* showing firemen clambering on ladders to fight a fire there. The accompanying story said that the house had caught fire because of overloaded electrical circuits. No one was injured, but the three-story building was gutted by flames, according to the story. It made me heartsick to see the sorry end of "1619." A few months later, the city razed what remained of the house because it constituted a danger. When we drove past after that, there was only an empty lot where "1619" had stood, but in recent years a small shopping center was constructed there. The whole neighborhood now is ugly and depressing.

Mama knew nothing of "1619's" sad fate. She seemed quite content at William's, but her health continued to go downhill, and she had to spend more and more time in bed. It became necessary to get a 24-hour nurse to stay with her. It was very difficult for William. There was no extra bedroom for the nurse. She slept on a cot in Mama's room. Someone had to be in the room with Mama at night because she often needed to use the bedpan — or thought she needed it. William slept with one eye open, fearing the nurse might not hear Mama's call. He told me he sometimes drank some wine to get a little rest. He had no privacy whatever during those years with the nurse or someone else always around. When we came on weekends to relieve William, Dan slept on the couch and Jane slept at Taft's with Geraldine. Since the nurse was off duty, I watched over Mama from the cot in her room. She was so fearful of soiling the bed she called for the bedpan seven or eight times a night. Even on the nights when we were there, William always got home by 9, though I urged him to take more time for himself. He would get a haircut, have dinner out, and, occasionally, go to a movie. Yet he never complained or was irritable. It was difficult to find nurses for 24-hour duty; we needed a practical nurse, not a registered nurse, one who would do a little cooking for Mama as well as look after her. Actually, Lillie and Holly did most of the cooking; one or both brought Chinese dishes every day. One of the nurses almost killed Mama. One morning, she carelessly threw a burning cigarette or match into a wastebasket near Mama's bed. When Holly arrived, the house smelled of smoke, and all the doors were open. Mama had suffered another small stroke and was unable to talk.

"Her eyes were so big and scared, and she pointed to the wastebasket," Holly recalled. The nurse had burned her hand putting out the fire, which fortunately was confined to the wastebasket. It enraged us to think of how terrified Mama must have been as she saw the flames in the wastebasket and was unable to move or speak to get help. The fire could so easily have caught onto the bedclothes. The nurse probably smelled the smoke just in time. Knowing she would be fired, she quit. Mama never spoke of the incident after she regained her speech. That was when we hired Ann, the last nurse, an older woman who took better care of Mama than any of the others.

One Sunday morning Mama was suddenly stricken very ill. William and I were frightened and called Dr. Chuck immediately. He said Mama had had a heart attack and must go to the hospital. Mama had never been in a hospital, and we knew it would be a devastating experience for her. The family arranged that one of us would be with her around the clock so she would never wake up and find herself alone in a strange place. She knew little English and couldn't communicate with the doctors or nurses. Lillie and Holly brought her Chinese food. She wouldn't have eaten the American meals. She stayed in the hospital, White Memorial, a couple of weeks.

Mama recovered from the heart attack, but her general condition weakened. She was completely bedridden, but was never senile. She still read her Chinese newspapers and watched TV. Her favorite program was "Queen For a Day." On Saturday nights, I sat with her as we watched Sid Ceasar. Even though she didn't understand much of what was said, she laughed at the antics. Most of all, she loved seeing her grandchildren and great-grandchildren. Each time one of them came, he or she went first to Ah Po's bedroom to greet her. Ah Po always had a *lai see* to give them. She didn't know that after the children had respectfully said *dah jeh* (thank you), they returned the *lai see* to William to be recycled when other grandchildren visited. It was a harmless deception, and it made Mama happy to give something to the children, just as she had always done.

Holly and Ed built a spacious home overlooking Silver Lake, a few blocks from Lillie's. There was plenty of room for their family of four children, and it was ideally suited for entertaining, which Holly loved. When the house was still quite new, Holly wanted Mama to stay with her for a while to give William a rest. Mama consented, and Holly made her most comfortable in the downstairs rumpus room overlooking the garden. After just two days, Mama wanted to go back to William's, but she did settle down and stay about a month.

During the last year of her illness, Mama got very thin; she had never weighed more than 90 pounds, but now she was so light that Holly said she could lift her. She wore her hair in a long braid; it was my job to braid it. Her hair remained healthy, long and thick, black streaked with gray. She didn't suffer much pain, but it was frustrating for her to be helpless and bedridden. Sometimes she would sigh and say *say joong ho* (death would be better). The last weekend in October, 1957, was the last weekend of her life. She was noticeably weak but not in pain. I brought her dinner on a tray on Saturday night as usual. She had always eaten unassisted, but she seemed too tired to eat, so I fed her. That night she slept better than usual, not calling for the bedpan as often. Sunday, she seemed half asleep, but I fed her a breakfast of hot cereal. William and I were very concerned. Taft came over (he always came to see Mama every day) and we decided to have Dr. Chuck come. I fed Mama her lunch, her last meal. I talked to her, and she tried to answer, but could only mumble. After lunch she fell into a deep sleep, like a coma. Dr. Chuck examined her and then asked William if he minded if Mama died in his house or if he wanted her transferred to a hospital. (Some Chinese think it's bad luck if someone dies in their home.) Of course, William said he wanted her to stay home. There was nothing Dr. Chuck could do for her. When he left, we had the impression Mama could linger like that for days or weeks. Somehow, none of us felt that death was imminent. Still, I hated to go home, but Ann was due to return, and the children had to go to school. Mama was still sleeping when I left. The next morning toward noon, Lucy phoned. She said Mama had died, that Ann had checked on her and later had found she had stopped breathing. I felt both grief and relief because I knew Mama had long wanted to die. She was 81. It was October 27, 1957.

I immediately drove to William's, numb and in a sort of daze. Saddest of all to me was that Mama died alone. One of us had been with her most of the time during her illness, but when she died, none of us was there. William had gone to work that morning, though he had almost stayed home, he said. When he was told at work that there was a phone call for him, he knew immediately what it was. When I got to William's, most of the family was there — I lived the furthest away. Ann had prepared Mama so that she looked as though she was asleep, and told us we should go and see her before the morticians came. Lillie, Holly, and I went in first. Mama looked peaceful, but she was very white. I told myself, and still want to believe, that she died in her sleep and didn't know she was alone. We sisters went into the kitchen because we couldn't bear to see the hearse arrive and take Mama away. Later, I went with Taft and William to the mortuary to choose a casket and make funeral arrangements.

In order to give relatives outside of Los Angeles time to assemble, the funeral was set for a week later. The immediate family gathered at William's to go to the funeral; even the smallest children were somber and quiet. I took a quick glance at Mama in her casket and had to look away because the morticians had applied makeup so that it didn't even look like Mama. We followed the usual Chinese ritual of distributing money and candy to those who attended the funeral. Mama was buried next to Papa at Rosedale Cemetery, a most dismal place. That night there was the big dinner for relatives at a Chinatown restaurant.

With Mama's death, the heart of the family was gone, but Lillie and Holly kept the family together. We celebrated birthdays and holidays at one or another of their homes, but we didn't get together nearly as often as we had when Mama was alive. Now both Papa and Mama, the founders of our clan, were gone. It was truly the end of one era and the beginning of another for the Leung family.

Epilogue

As I write this in September, 1987, Papa and Mama's six surviving sons and daughters are well into old age. Mincie, the youngest, is 70 and I, the oldest, am 82. Howard enjoys his bartendering job and works four nights a week. Taft still does some accounting. Mincie has an ideal design for living — teaching a few hours a week at Cal State Northridge for six months, and spending the other six months in Honolulu, where he can be found every day at the beach at Waikiki. The rest of us are retired. William died in 1968, and Lillie, in 1973.

Our extended family now numbers 55, with another on the way. Papa, especially, and Mama, to a lesser degree, would be astonished at what has transpired with the Leungs since they came to Gold Mountain from Sweet Bamboo at the turn of the century. We are into the fifth generation and are now an international family. Most of the third and fourth generations have married Caucasians. Intermarriage has long since ceased to be a scandal; it is taken for granted. The Caucasians who have married into the family have been happily and comfortably absorbed into the clan. As for the rest of us, few can speak or read Chinese. Some of us don't even look Chinese. Our Chinese forebears have receded further and further into the past. Our heritage seems very far away. The little ones of the fourth and fifth generations probably feel entirely American. Perhaps these pages will stir their interest in our ancestry and roots so far across the sea.

Postscript

Return to Sweet Bamboo

JANE LEUNG LARSON

It has been more than ten years since *Sweet Bamboo* was first published, but at its heart, the Tom Leung family has not changed greatly. This may be because Holly, 88, gathers the family together every Thanksgiving and Christmas in her home and keeps in touch with those of us in distant places with long phone calls. She, Howard, and Monroe are the three surviving children of Tom Leung and Wong Bing Woo in 2001, with the deaths of my mother, Louise, in 1988, Taft in 1989, and Mincie in 1990. The extended family is now 71 strong, and most still live in Southern California. So far, Holly has been the only second-generation member who has lived to hold her fifth-generation great grandchild in her arms.

As we in the third generation have grown older, we have found our own ways of preserving our family history and creating new traditions. Kirby Leung, Monroe's eldest son, has long been interested in the family's history, even decorating his living room with old photographs, T. Leung Herb Company plaques, and a framed display of his grandfather's silk robe. So, in 1999, when he realized that Tom Leung had first landed in America one hundred years earlier, he decided to invite the whole family to his home to celebrate the occasion. He marveled what a different family the Tom Leungs had become, in many ways indistinguishable from other Americans in diet, language, and culture — yet still quite conscious of being Chinese.

But at what point will we cease feeling Chinese? One third of Tom Leung's descendants are now of mixed ethnicity, combining European or Japanese ancestry with Chinese, and all twelve of the fifth-generation children are of mixed Chinese and European blood. My mother's four great grandchildren are only one-eighth Chinese. The only Chinese words most of the younger generations know are the useful Cantonese "toilet" expressions that can be spoken out loud to one's children in public places.

For me, a child of the Tom Leung family's first mixed marriage, my Chinese background has always been important. My brothers and I considered our mother's Chinese relatives our only family because we never met our father's Swedish American relatives; his parents had disowned him when he married my mother. As I grew up, my father impressed upon me that I was special because I was half Chinese. So, perhaps it was only natural that I would feel Chinese, although most people don't recognize me as such. My two brothers, on the other hand, have been much less preoccupied with their Chinese identity, perhaps because they have lived much more of their lives in Los Angeles as part of the family, whereas I left when I was 17. Searching for myself, I made "China" my life, from my work for the Northwest China Council in Oregon and similar groups in New York, to my avocations, studying Chinese and digging into our family's Chinese history.

Another family member has delved into the meaning of being Chinese American in her own way. My cousin Cherylene Lee, Holly's youngest daughter, is a nationally known playwright living in San Francisco whose work deals almost exclusively with Chinese American themes: *Carry the Tiger to the Mountain*, about the murder of Vincent Chin in Detroit by two unemployed autoworkers who thought he was Japanese; *The Ballad of Doc Hay*, about a famous Chinese herbalist in Eastern Oregon, with much ambiance coming directly from Tom Leung's "How to Get Well and Keep Well"; and *Lost Vegas Acts*, a semi-autobiographical musical about three Chinese American sisters and their father in 1960s show business. Cherylene and her sister Virginia were child actresses, and most of their roles played upon their Asian American background. She reflects, "When I was growing up and performing, I didn't realize how much being Chinese American influenced the roles I was given to play in TV or movies or on the stage. Today as a writer, I find I write mostly about the Chinese American perspective. . . . One of the things which fascinates me is what aspects of Chinese culture are passed on through generations and what aspects are lost in the process of being American. That is probably at the core of my writing."

In the years since my mother wrote *Sweet Bamboo*, we have uncovered much more of our history and our roots, including meeting our relatives in Sweet Bamboo.

When Taft's widow, Esther, moved from her home into a condo, she gave Tom Leung's classical Chinese library to the Chinese American Museum and UCLA's East Asian Library, thousands of clothbound and hand-stitched volumes that had been stored in her garage untouched for at least 50 years. Among the other treasures found were Tom's well-thumbed, handwritten herbal prescription book and four framed poems calligraphed by Kang Yu-wei to Tom Leung, including the one that appears in *Sweet Bamboo* and was believed by my mother to have been lost.

In 1998, Tom Leung's papers from the Society to Protect the Emperor (Bo Wong) were published in China to coincide with the 100th anniversary of the Hundred Days of Reform of Kang Yu-wei and Emperor Kuang-hsu. Tom Leung had kept hundreds of letters from his Bo Wong days, a unique collection because he had many personal letters from Kang Yu-wei and Liang Ch'i-ch'ao, as well as correspondence with Association members all over the world. After Tom's death in 1931, none of his children took much interest in these materials because they couldn't read Chinese. When the family sold their home (1619) in the 1950s, they left the letters behind. My father, by this time divorced from my mother, secretly salvaged them, along with many other historical artifacts from the vacant house, and gave them to the Southwest Museum. When he died in 1981, my mother reclaimed the items at the Southwest Museum and gave the letters to UCLA's East Asian Library. The letters were copied for me, and I began to work with Charles Liu to get them translated into English.

What started as a translation project became an inexhaustible field of research as I came to realize that the Bo Wong was a remarkable organization that had played an important role in Chinese political development. However, hardly any historians in the U.S. now study it, and I had to go to China to find people who could help me interpret the historical meaning of the documents. James Cheng, head of UCLA's East Asian Library, sent microfilms of the whole Tom Leung collection to the Chinese scholars, and in 1998 Fang Zhiqin of the Guangdong Academy of Social Science published the papers. My grandfather's impulse to save the old letters and my father's salvaging of them had provided scholars with new material for the study of early Chinese reformers.

History began to come together in a more personal way when I decided to go back to Sweet Bamboo and find our relatives. My mother had never wanted to meet our relatives in China; remembering how her mother complained about them writing for money, she feared that they would expect the same from us. So she was content with visiting the Gum Jook hydraulic power plant, imagining the villages her parents had lived in nearly a hundred years ago. But after my mother died, my third cousin Edith Tom, the daughter of E Sow (my mother's second cousin's wife), went back to Gum Jook to meet the remaining Toms. She found that Sun Duck now was one of the most prosperous counties in all of China, with our relatives among those who were doing well.

So in 1990, I returned to Gum Jook, the first of Tom Leung's descendants to meet the Toms on their home soil, bringing my mother's book as a gift. Our common ancestor with the Gum Jook Toms was Tom Leung's father, Tan Zizhong, who was a man of some renown, having passed the very top palace examinations to win the *jinshi* degree (the equivalent of a doctorate) and become a magistrate in Hunan. Tan Zizhong had a second wife whose surviving son, Tom Joe Yuet (Tan Zuyue), still lived in the village with his eldest son (an accountant), in the same narrow lane that Tom Leung came from. But now the homes were new two- and three-story buildings with roof gardens, and Tom Joe Yuet's sons owned motorcycles and trucks. I was hosted by the middle son, Runting, a chainsmoking wheeler-dealer who lived in the nearby town of Longjiang (Dragon River, by that power plant that my mother and I visited in

1977). Runting was deputy manager of the town's beer company, whose brand was Dragon Power beer. He told me that many valuable scrolls and other possessions had been confiscated from the family during the Cultural Revolution because they had overseas relatives. The family's *jiapu*, or family tree, had long ago been lost. Sadly, it seemed that I knew more about the family history than they did.

Then, in 1996, I met many of my grandmother Wong Bing Woo's relatives in Hong Kong and Guangdong. The Overseas Chinese Affairs Office in Guangzhou tracked them all down for me from the last letter sent to my grandmother in 1939 by her family. In Hong Kong, I met Samuel Wong, son of Bui Hing Go, who had created such an impression among the Leung kids when he boldly went to USC dances and dated beautiful Caucasian women. Sam, a retired accountant and avid tennis player and golfer, told me that after his father left USC in 1922, he went to Columbia University and graduated in 1924. When Bui Hing Go returned to China, he became the chief translator for Shell Oil Asia in Shanghai. Later, he took up accounting and moved to Hong Kong, where he died in 1949. Sam had visited his relatives in Guangdong a few times and even owned a house there, the only building still standing of the Wong family's ten-building compound, but occupied by non-family members who had taken over all the Wong buildings after 1949. Sam, like me, is fascinated by the family's history and our connections; he remembers when Mincie visited his father in Shanghai during the war. In 1999, Lillie's daughter Patricia and Taft's daughter Geraldine also met Sam in Hong Kong.

I found that the Wongs in Sun Duck had suffered far more from the Communist Revolution than the Toms because of their landlord background, losing their property and getting little education. The Wongs who stayed in Gum Jook had become peasants, whereas the enterprising and relatively sophisticated Toms made their livings in the dynamic market town nearby. Before going into the countryside, I called Uncle Peitian in Canton. He had retired from a fountain pen factory, looked a bit like Uncle William, and has a daughter living in Australia. Matter of factly accepting my word that he and I were relatives, he took my husband and me deep into "the lanes" of old Canton to meet his sister and niece, who lived simply but comfortably, with the once unattainable home telephone and a new audio system. Peitian and his niece helped us rent a van, and we drove to the village to visit the Yo Tan relatives. As we walked through the door to Aunt Xuefei's front room, the small television set next to the family's large ancestral shrine was blaring Whoopie Goldberg, who was emceeing the Academy Awards live from Hollywood, thanks to Hong Kong television! Aside from such cultural collision, the three Wong sisters and their families lived much as farmers always have in the Pearl River delta, an area rich in bananas, rice, and fish. They still had old houses but, with profits from their fish pond, were soon to move into new ones. We pored over *Sweet Bamboo* and a family tree, but they didn't know the name of their grandfather, so we never figured out our common relative. My husband and I were welcomed into this family with a huge hot pot lunch, featuring special Sun Duck dumplings and the freshest fish possible straight from the pond.

Someday, when we have the time and leisure, I hope my cousins and brothers will return with me to Sweet Bamboo, accompanied by our new-found Hong Kong cousin, Sam.

Mamie Louise Leung Larson

Sweet Bamboo tells the story of the Tom Leung family, but it gives only a hint of the life of the author, Mamie Louise Leung Larson. Mamie was born on February 16, 1905, in Los Angeles. Soon afterwards, the family received a special guest, the famous reformer Kang Yu-Wei, who was exiled from China and was Tom Leung's former teacher and political ally. In a 1934 *Los Angeles Times Sunday Magazine* article on Kang Yu-Wei, Mamie wrote, "I have a very personal souvenir of Kang's visit. It is my Chinese name. For three months I remained anonymous while my parents awaited the coming of the great scholar. This little one has no name, my father told Kang. Would you honor us by giving her one? Kang smiled 'Let it be Lau Lan, after the most famous woman of France, Joan of Arc.' "

Strong-willed, intelligent, and with an adventurous streak, Mamie grew up to be a pioneer among Chinese-American women. She became the first Asian American reporter for a major American newspaper when she was hired, at age 21, by the *Los Angeles Record* on July 15, 1926. She had just graduated with Phi Beta Kappa from the University of Southern California. Her first article, written for a USC journalism class, was a front-page story on the month-old *(mun-yurt)* party for her nephew. Working for the *Record*, she single-handedly had to cover the grand jury and superior courts, the D.A.'s office, and the sheriff's department, as well as elections. Mamie loved her new job and excelled at it, much to the surprise of her colleagues on other papers, who couldn't imagine her toughing it out. Her first big story was the lurid divorce case involving Charlie Chaplin.

She left the *Record* in 1929, but her newspaper career continued into the 1940's with stints at the *San Francisco News, Chicago Daily Times, Los Angeles Times Sunday Magazine,* and *Los Angeles Daily News.* Some of her most memorable stories included events such as the tax-evasion trial of Al Capone, Albert Einstein's national crusade for disarmament, and Madame

Chiang Kai-shek's United States' trip to raise funds for China's fight against Japan. She interviewed Capone several times.

After she moved to Chicago in 1929, she married fellow reporter Arnold (Wolf) Larson without the knowledge of her family, and in 1930 had her first child, Stan. Eventually the Leungs lovingly accepted Arnold into their clan. Mamie and Arnold moved to Topanga Canyon in 1940 and began to build a home in an area without roads, water, or electricity. This could not have been easy for her since she was used to the conveniences of the Leung household. She came to love Topanga for its quiet, rural isolation, and her individualistic neighbors accepted her without prejudice although she was the only Asian there for many years. Two more children were born, Jane in 1945 and Dan in 1948. Arnold and Mamie separated in the early 1950's, but Mamie continued to raise her young children alone in isolated Topanga.

Not knowing how to drive, she survived by working at telephone soliciting, finding customers for a local roofing contractor. Eventually, she saved enough to buy her first automobile, and then hired a local handyman to teach her how to drive it; Mamie was more than fifty years old at the time!

In 1958, after many years away from her profession, Mamie joined the *Santa Monica Evening Outlook* to cover the Malibu and Topanga area, a beat she developed. She was particularly proud of a series she wrote on a hotly debated nuclear power plant proposed for Corral Canyon, in Malibu. The series was praised by both sides in the struggle. During her years as a reporter, she kept her opinions to herself, but upon retirement in 1975, she began to write "OpEd" articles to the editor for the *Los Angeles Times*, *Newsweek*, and local newspapers. Her scathing analyses on many topics, from Reagan administration policy on Nicaragua to brush burning regulations in Topanga, revealed her sharp wit and intellect.

It was during these later years that Mamie was able to fulfill her desire to travel. She startled friends and family by traveling throughout Mexico with her two children on a bus. That was a trip not often attempted in 1962. She also visited Canada, Europe, and Asia.

As a child, she was made to take Chinese lessons, but managed to forget most of what she had learned. As an adult, living outside of the Chinese community, she spoke what little Chinese she knew only around her family. Throughout her childhood and early adulthood, she was very uncomfortable with her identity as a Chinese American, but Arnold's fascination with her heritage encouraged Mamie to embrace her Chineseness. She wrote many articles such as "Please, What Am I? Chinese or American?" — a cover story in the *Los Angeles Times Sunday Magazine* (November 4, 1934). She was one of the first Chinese Americans to visit China, in May 1976, and she returned three more times with her daughter, visiting Gum Jook, the family village, in 1977.

Among the honors Mamie received were the Pioneer Woman's Award of the Chinese Historical Society of Southern California (1978), the Woman Warrior Award for lifetime achievement from the Asian-Pacific Women's Network (1983), a California State Senate Resolution honoring her contributions to journalism (1983), a commendation from Los Angeles Mayor Tom Bradley (1984), a plaque from the California State University cultural exhibition, "Chinese Women of America: 1934-1982" (1984), and, just three weeks before her death, an award for her role as a pioneering journalist from the Asian American Journalists Association (1988).

She died in Topanga, in her sleep, on October 1, 1988.

— *The Larson Family*

The Tom Leung Family Tree

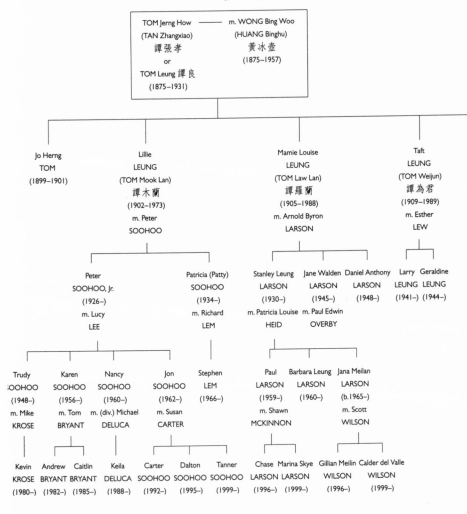

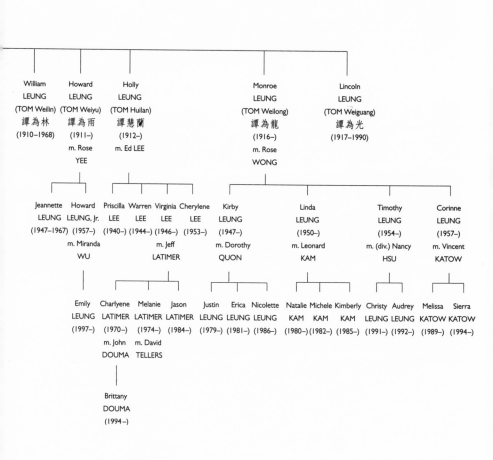

William
LEUNG
(TOM Weilin)
譚為林
(1910–1968)

Howard
LEUNG
(TOM Weiyu)
譚為雨
(1911–)
m. Rose
YEE

Holly
LEUNG
(TOM Huilan)
譚慧蘭
(1912–)
m. Ed LEE

Monroe
LEUNG
(TOM Weilong)
譚為龍
(1916–)
m. Rose
WONG

Lincoln
LEUNG
(TOM Weiguang)
譚為光
(1917–1990)

Jeannette
LEUNG
(1947–1967)
m. Miranda
WU

Howard
LEUNG, Jr.
(1957–)

Priscilla
LEE
(1940–)

Warren
LEE
(1944–)

Virginia
LEE
(1946–)
m. Jeff
LATIMER

Cherylene
LEE
(1953–)

Kirby
LEUNG
(1947–)
m. Dorothy
QUON

Linda
LEUNG
(1950–)
m. Leonard
KAM

Timothy
LEUNG
(1954–)
m. (div.) Nancy
HSU

Corinne
LEUNG
(1957–)
m. Vincent
KATOW

Emily
LEUNG
(1997–)

Charlyene
LATIMER
(1970–)
m. John
DOUMA

Melanie
LATIMER
(1974–)
m. David
TELLERS

Jason
LATIMER
(1984–)

Justin
LEUNG
(1979–)

Erica
LEUNG
(1981–)

Nicolette
LEUNG
(1986–)

Natalie
KAM
(1980–)

Michele
KAM
(1982–)

Kimberly
KAM
(1985–)

Christy
LEUNG
(1991–)

Audrey
LEUNG
(1992–)

Melissa
KATOW
(1989–)

Sierra
KATOW
(1994–)

Brittany
DOUMA
(1994–)

Glossary

ROMANIZATION	MEANING	CHINESE
Ah Jieh	sister	亞娣
Ah Po	grandmother; an old woman	亞婆
Bo Wong	Empire Reform Society	保皇會
Bok Foo	paternal uncle	伯父
bok gway	white ghosts	白鬼
bow	bun (a type of dim sum)	包
bun long	betel nut	檳榔
cha jay	a Chinese shampoo	茶仔
cho	smelly	臭
cho gway	low-class ghosts	粗鬼
da bin low	chafing dish	打邊爐
dah jeh	"many thanks"	多謝
dan gway	orange flower	丹桂
di daum	courageous	大胆

ROMANIZATION	MEANING	CHINESE
dim sum	Chinese tea cakes	點 心
do sa	black bean paste	豆 沙
dong gwa	melon	冬 瓜
E Bok Foo	second paternal uncle	二 伯 父
E Bok Mo	E Bok Foo's wife	二 伯 母
E Goo Jeh	second cousin	二 姑 姐
E Gow	second cousin	二 哥
E Sow	second cousin's wife	二 嫂
fan jui	a crust of toasted rice	飯 焦
fo yer	salted bean curd	腐 乳
fung-shui	geomancy	風 水
fung sup	"wind wet" or rheumatism	風 濕
gay don go	steamed egg cake	雞 蛋 糕
gee mah woo	black sesame seed pudding	芝 蔴 糊
Gee Yut	the Day of Knowing	知 日
gip see	a concubine	妾 侍
go hing	merry	高 興
gong gways	laborers	工 鬼
gong hay fat choy	"congratulations and be prosperous" (a Chinese New Year greeting)	恭 喜 發 財
Goo Mah	nurse or paternal aunt	姑 媽
goon	an official	官
goong gways	poor ghosts	窮 鬼
gum cho	a Chinese herb	甘 草
gum hee	gold jewelry	金 器
gum jo fan lay	"home so early?"	咁 早 返 來
Gum Jook	Sweet Bamboo	甘 竹
gwa	Chinese squash	瓜
gwa choy	melon and vegetable	瓜 菜
gwa lay	"come here"	過 來

ROMANIZATION	MEANING	CHINESE
gwa lo op	Peking roast duck	掛爐鴨
gway	ghosts	鬼
gway lo	old ghosts	鬼佬
hah mai	dried shrimp	蝦米
hak gway	black ghosts	黑鬼
ho sun foo	very much suffering	好辛苦
ho tahn	very luxurious	好聽
Hong Sing Sung	teacher Hong (Kang Yu-wei)	康先生
hoong fong	red room	紅房
Jew gways	Jewish ghosts	猶太鬼
jick huek	"go immediately"	直去
Jo Tan	left bank	左灘
jook	rice gruel (porridge)	粥
joong	Chinese tamale	粽
jung gwat	pound bones	揉骨
Kang Yu-wei	a scholar who advocated political reform in China (1858–1927)	康有為
King Joy Low	name of a restaurant	瓊彩樓
Kit King Louis (Lei Jieqiong)	personal name	雷洁瓊
Kuang-Hsu	reigning title of emperor Tsai-t'ien (1871–1908)	光緒
Kwan Yin	goddess of mercy	觀音
Kwangtung	a province in China (Guangdong)	廣東
lai see	monetary gift wrapped in red	利是
Law Lan	pink flower; personal name	羅蘭
Liang Chi-chao	one of the major advocates of political reform in China (1873–1929)	梁啓超
lily feet	bound feet	纏足
lop cherng	Chinese sausage	腊腸

ROMANIZATION	MEANING	CHINESE
lun jun	clumsy and slow	論盡
mah jongg	mahjong	麻雀
Mook Lan	a Chinese heroine (woman warrior)	木蘭
mui jay	maid (little sister)	妹仔
mun yirt	month-old	滿月
mung jung	cross or irritable	猛掙
naw mai	sweet rice	糯米
Ng Gow	fifth cousin	五哥
nir hok sung	girl scholar (student)	女學生
Sahm Gow	third cousin	三哥
Sahm yup	three districts of Guangdong, China	三邑
Say Gow	fourth brother	四哥
say joong ho	"death would be better"	死更好
Say yup	four districts of Guangdong, China	四邑
Sit Gum Kum	a person's name	薛錦琴
sui song	smiling death	笑喪
sui yea	nighttime snack	宵夜
Sun Duck	a district in China	順德
Sup E Tai Bo	a dose of herbs	十二太保
Ta-t'ung Shu	*Book of the Great Community*	大同書
	by Kang Yu-wei	
tahn	"take it easy"	賒
tai dee sai yun	"see the Western people"	睇得西人
tit da jo	a pungent liquid that relieves pain	鐵打油
Tom Cherng How	personal name	譚張孝
Tom Foo Yuen	personal name	譚富園
Tom How Wing	personal name	譚效榮
Tom Leung	personal name	譚良
Tom She Bin	personal name	譚樹彬
tong	Chinese organizations	堂

ROMANIZATION	MEANING	CHINESE
tong chong	Chinese clothes	唐裝
tsai	an assortment of vegetables	菜
Tzu-hsi	Empress Dowager (1836–1908)	慈禧太后
um pa cho	not ashamed	唔怕醜
um sai jang	"we needn't quarrel"	(唔)勿使爭
union gways	union ghosts	工會鬼
Wong Bing Woo	personal name	黃冰壺
Wong Che Tat	personal name	黃處達
Wong Gways	yellow ghosts	黃鬼
Yang Kuei Fei	concubine of Hsuan Tsung of the Tang Dynasty (719–756)	楊貴妃
yer yo	"Thousand Wonders Oil"	意油
yern say	Chinese parsley (coriander)	芫茜
yin wah	bird's nest soup	燕窩
yir sang	raw fish	魚生
Yo tan	right bank	右灘
yum sum cha	heart tea (ginseng tea)	飲心茶
yup yerk	"fill the prescriptions"	執藥